Preaching
for
Recovery
in a
Strife-torn
Church

Preaching
for
Recovery
in a
Strife-torn
Church

JERRIEN GUNNINK

**Ministry
Resources
Library**

Zondervan Publishing House • Grand Rapids, MI

MINISTRY RESOURCES LIBRARY is an imprint of Zondervan Publishing House, 1415 Lake Drive, S.E., Grand Rapids, Michigan 49506.

Edited by Joan Johnson

Library of Congress Cataloging-in-Publication Data

Gunnink, Jerrien, 1928–
    Preaching for recovery in a strife-torn church / Jerrien Gunnink.
       p.   cm.
    Bibliography: p.
    ISBN 0-310-31121-7
    1. Preaching. 2. Church controversies. 3. Church renewal. I. Title.
BV4221.G86   1989   89-35847
251—dc20   CIP

Printed in the United States of America

89 90 91 92 93 94 / CH / 10 9 8 7 6 5 4 3 2 1

To Ida,
who tends to my traumas
with love and patience

Contents

Foreword

It isn't every day that a pastor finds a book that provides real help for his preaching ministry. Here is one!

Ministers everywhere face the problem of preaching to shattered churches. Author Gunnink says, "No one ever prepared me for this kind of preaching in homiletics class." Most likely no one prepared you for the task either. But Dr. Gunnink does. He has hammered out a scriptural method for preaching to a church splintered and torn.

He speaks with credibility, since his suggestions stem from his own experience with a strife-torn church. God blessed Gunnink's years of struggle, trial and error, and intensive Bible study by healing that congregation so that it is healthy and growing. Only last year Dr. Gunnink was able to start a new work because he felt the task with the divided church was accomplished. Gunnink's words and life speak with great authority.

But this book is not just for the pastor of a troubled church. If your church is not strife-torn, we can certainly thank God. But it is also appropriate to examine whether your current attitude and behavior is working for good or ill. Perhaps you are sowing the seeds of division without realizing it. Perhaps you are unknowingly contributing to factions among your own people. Dr. Gunnink incisively examines the heart of the preacher and its effects on the flock.

Dr. Gunnink's book does not merely report the experience of one man in one congregation. To fulfill the requirements of the Doctor of Ministry program at Westminster Theological Seminary in California for which *Preaching for*

Recovery in a Strife-Torn Church was prepared, Pastor Gunnink surveyed ministers from a large number of strife-torn
churches and numerous denominational officials acquainted
with all too many such situations.

He draws heavily upon their accumulated scriptural
insights. In these pages, therefore, you will find biblical
wisdom in practical form, cogently written, to guide you past
the treacherous shoals that have wrecked many a well-meant,
but ill-conceived preaching ministry. Pastor—buy this book
and follow it closely!

JAY E. ADAMS
Director, the Doctor of Ministry Program
Westminster Theological Seminary
Escondido, California

Preface

At least ten percent of the churches in the United States and Canada are presently embroiled in internal conflict so large that their witness has been nullified. This was the estimate of church leaders contacted in a recent survey I conducted in these countries. There are 310,000 Protestant congregations in America, according to Dr. Win Arn, founder of the American Institute of Church Growth. This suggests that more than 30,000 Protestant churches in the United States alone are in a serious conflict at any given time. This alarming phenomenon has caused denominational executives to search for new ways to alleviate strife in the local church.

A new genre of specialists has emerged, with the purpose of leading a church through dissension and resolving the internal conflict. Troubled churches are led through "assertiveness training," "negotiating sessions," "communication techniques," "listening skills," "confrontational methods," "peacemaking," and a host of other formulas designed to bring harmony and peace.

These third-party consultants can be valuable in planning a strategy to resolve a church fight. Understanding the dynamics of pastoral counseling in dealing with troublesome people is also helpful. The Bible clearly informs us how to resolve things with our fellow Christians in an acceptable manner (Matt. 18).

This book does not intend to minimize such efforts to lessen the tension in a church. These approaches have their value. But there is a glaring omission in the literature on conflict-resolution. Nowhere is the topic of preaching as a healing agent examined closely. Dr. Speed Leas, a leading authority on church conflict resolution and the author of a number of books on the subject, wrote that very little thought has been given to "the relationship between preaching and conflict management, and there certainly is very little literature on this." A comprehensive review of the books on the subject confirmed the statement.

This book is written to try to fill that void. I firmly believe that a church wounded by conflict needs a remedy that includes preaching to experience a full recovery. This belief does not minimize the importance of other aspects of the healing process; rather, it maximizes the significance of preaching in that process. All parts are needed.

Without apology, I assume that preaching is a central facet of the life of a congregation. When properly and enthusiastically handled, preaching can affect and heal a church. I have seen it happen.

Eleven years ago I began ministering to a torn church without any guidance and direction. I was simply on my own, using whatever God-given abilities I possessed. Through these years I have learned what can be accomplished through preaching and what the limitations are. If these are not clearly understood, the pastor may become totally frustrated and the church may become more damaged. I offer, then, the following pages, the result of my research on the subject combined with my personal parish experiences, as a guide to all who seek to preach for recovery.

Introduction

Pastor, this church is a grand mess! I didn't think anybody would ever come to a place with all the problems we have. I feel sorry for you." This is not the warmest welcome a person could receive, but it is exactly what met me when the van was unloaded in front of the new parsonage.

The church I was to serve had just endured a painful experience. One pastor, who had served the congregation for eight years, left with a number of members to form a new congregation. The stated reason for the split was a difference in "philosophy of ministry." A co-pastor, who embraced the same philosophy as the first, was politely eased out of the church. Parishioners who left were labeled "the troublemakers." Some thought this exodus had solved all their problems. Others knew better.

"It's a terrible shame," one said. "The minister was dishonest," claimed another. "We are the talk of the community and it sure feels embarrassing," a lady stated. Friends became strangers, a cold chill descended on the congregation, alienation set in. The church was in a state of shock from its deep wounds. Some people were hurt by arguments, misunderstandings, cutting remarks. Others were angry, confused, bewildered.

The church was depressed. "How could this happen to us?" "What did we do wrong?" "What could we have done to prevent it?" These and similar questions found their way into nearly every conversation. A thoughtful member told me, "This division will set the church back ten years." Families stopped coming to church; others became inactive or transferred to other churches. Young people asked hard questions about "loving each other," "forgiveness," and "being one in the Lord." Some dismissed the church altogether.

The task before me seemed overwhelming. I was deluged with my own questions. What could I do to help? How could I approach this hurting, bleeding church? I knew my preaching would be essential for recovery, but on what should I preach? How would I preach? What topics would I be wise to avoid? Should I tackle the issues directly or do so slowly and carefully? No one had prepared me for this kind of preaching in homiletics class.

Since my abilities and gifts lie in preaching, I decided that I would have to do most of the rebuilding and healing through the use of that gift. But to do so I would have to give careful thought to the kind of preaching that heals, so my preaching itself wouldn't produce more conflict. Over time—and after many painful episodes—I developed a preaching approach that helped heal the church, one that met the needs of people. But this approach does not limit itself to the church I served. No, the principles and the process I struggled to apprehend and then practice could be powerful for any strife-torn church. This is why I've written the book. You could call it a handbook on preaching for recovery.

But what is a strife-torn church? You know the answer to that if you have been in one! Yet you may not be able to articulate it. Let me describe it. A strife-torn church is one in which the level of internal conflict is so great that it no longer fulfills its mission and calling in the world. It is wounded, hurting, divided. It can be roughly compared to a cancer patient whose surgery necessitates complete rest. Chemotherapy, physical therapy, and other therapies will be needed to regain wholeness and strength. In the meantime, the patient is weak, immobile, and needy. Likewise, a strife-torn church dissipates energy dealing with the conflict so that there is little left for ministry to the world. It becomes ineffective in its witness. "Don't go to that church—it has lots of troubles," people say. Newcomers to the area shy away from a church they know is in conflict: "Isn't that the church with all the troublemakers?" The church itself becomes introspective, filled with self-pity ("this shouldn't happen to us"), and painfully self-centered.

How can such a church be brought back to vitality and health? The answer to that question is the focus of this book. If you are one of those thousands of ministers who must mount the pulpit each Sunday and preach to a divided, splintered, fighting, exhausted congregation, this book is for you. Your church can recover; your preaching can be instrumental. That is the subject of the book.

In the present religious market there is a wide selection of books on church conflict. We can learn all we want about how to manage conflict wisely. Many of these books are valuable in helping us calm troubled waters, but to my knowledge none gives guidance for preaching to a church already divided.

Because I did not want to limit this book to my situation alone, I sent out a questionnaire to five hundred church leaders in fourteen different denominations to determine the various causes of division. A follow-up questionnaire went to pastors in splintered churches to determine how they handled situations like mine. The ideas and suggestions they offered are incorporated into the following pages.

I am grateful to all who responded and helped shape my thinking. I thank my former congregation for its patience and kindness in allowing me to conduct this study and write this book. Since the church has recovered from the split that occurred over eleven years ago, I am able to base my judgments on firsthand experience of God's blessing. I am grateful above all that the Holy Spirit used my preaching, which I believe was significant to that recovery.

Acknowledgments

I wish to acknowledge, with great appreciation, those who responded to my surveys, those who read the original manuscript, and those who offerd constructive criticisms. Those to whom I am especially indebted are Dr. Jay Adams, Dr. Ronald Nydam, the Rev. John Oldenburger, Jim Ritter, and my co-worker Dirk de Vries. I thank the First Christian Reformed Church of Denver for allowing me the privilege to serve them as senior pastor and the time for research and writing. I thank God for his healing of this church.

1

Preaching Is Pivotal

Perhaps you're skeptical that preaching is effective in resolving conflict. One pastor told me that "preaching cannot and does not produce healing of conflict in a church." Or maybe you think that preaching may have some value in conflict resolution, but that counseling group sessions and other facets of pastoral work are more vital.

Let me say at the outset that preaching is not done in a vacuum. An enormous amount of listening, talking, and caring needs to come before, after, and during the preaching of God's Word.

But preaching is a powerful healing agent that we've overlooked. God has given us a singularly potent therapy for healing. We need to take it. Our oversight is analogous to holding medicine that could heal our disease, but not choosing to swallow it. Preaching is unique in its curative power. I shall explain how.

Preaching Heals

A decimated congregation needs biblical preaching because it is a means of grace. As one writer says,

> The Bible is a means which the Holy Spirit employs for the extension of the church and for the edification and nourishment of the saints. Strictly speaking it is the Word

as it is preached in the name of God that is considered a means of grace.[1]

What does a church in conflict need more than nourishment and edification? What could better feed the church than a steady diet of God's Word? Preaching is a channel the Holy Spirit has chosen to change attitudes and behavior. People have often said to me, "Pastor, your sermons are helpful in bringing our congregation together. They are positive, encouraging, and instructive." This shows that they recognize preaching as a primary way to deal with divisions and conflict. Through preaching, the Holy Spirit changes lives. Paul says that the gospel came to the Thessalonians "not simply with words, but also with power, with the Holy Spirit and with deep conviction" (1 Thess. 1:5). The result of his preaching was changed lives.

A large church had gone through the agony of dismissing its pastor on a morals charge. Many had come to love the minister, an affable and creative man. They were deeply hurt when the truth of his indiscretion came to light. A minister noted for his preaching ability came to preach each Sunday. I visited this pastor and asked, "What did you do to restore this congregation?" He said, "The only thing I did was preach. I did no pastoral work, no teaching, and no administration." I said, "Do you actually believe preaching is so powerful that it can heal a church?" His reply was, "Definitely! And I have seen it happen!"

God uses preaching to convey his grace to people. The Holy Spirit not only converts people (Acts 16:14), but also changes their attitudes and behavior through preaching. After I had preached a series of sermons on 1 Corinthians 13, a man told me, "Now I know how to love my fellow church members, even my enemies." Preaching is a primary means of restoring the church.

The Occasion for Preaching

"I don't know if I want to go to church this morning," Ted said. "My stomach is in a knot and I have a terrible headache. There's a bunch of hypocrites and troublemakers in our church, and I can't worship with them." Mary sensed that Ted had trouble forgiving Jeff and his friends and hoped their paths would not cross at church. Jeff was an obnoxious, critical, negative person who seemed bent on stirring up trouble. The resultant atmosphere was tense. People wondered if there was any love left in the congregation. "But the Bible tells us not to give up meeting together," Mary said (see Heb. 10:25). For the sake of his wife and children, Ted consented to go.

When Ted entered the church he quickly glanced to see if Jeff or his friends were present. He had decided to sit wherever they weren't sitting. Then Ted discovered that the only vacant seat was directly behind Jeff. The usher led Ted to the spot. *This is horrible!* Ted thought. *How can I worship with this troublemaker sitting directly in front of me!* The organ began to play the moving strains of "Jesu, Joy of Man's Desiring." Ted focused his thoughts on the music. The words came to his mind, and he repeated them to himself. His anxieties subsided. The pastor pronounced the blessing of God and proceeded to say, "We are gathered before a holy God who is just and righteous. He is the great forgiver of sin, who calls us to confess our sins and receive the pardon he offers." Ted felt uneasy. The discomfort increased when the pastor read,

And do not grieve the Holy Spirit of God, with whom you were sealed for the day of redemption. Get rid of all bitterness, rage and anger, brawling and slander, along with every form of malice. Be kind and compassionate to one another, forgiving each other, just as in Christ God forgave you (Eph. 4:30–32).

Ted knew God had him cornered. His behavior and attitude were ungodly and he needed to confess his lovelessness. So Ted prayed, "Lord, please give me a forgiving heart just as you forgave me. Help me to have the proper attitude toward Jeff as well as others in the church who irritate me." When he finished, Ted felt different about the service. He eagerly anticipated the pastor's sermon on forgiveness. The Scripture for the morning was the fifth petition of the Lord's Prayer: "Forgive us our sins, for we also forgive everyone who sins against us" (Luke 11:4). Ted listened with rapt attention. *That's me,* he thought. *I've never had a forgiving spirit toward Jeff and I need to change.* Back home Ted thanked Mary for her encouragement.

When people gather for worship they sense that God is at the heart of their activity. This is key to understanding the unique efficacy of preaching. When the subject of conflict arises in the sermon, it does so in the context of their relationship to God and his declared will for their lives. In this setting, it is least threatening to deal with hurts, anger, and negative feelings toward others; it is easier to deal with the issues underlying the conflict. Worship provides a framework for people to resolve their hostilities as they hear the Word preached.

Two men I know had a long-standing feud with each other. They attended the same church, lived in the same community, and confessed the same Lord. The feud involved their children, a business venture, and finances. One Sunday I preached about how to forgive one another. At the conclusion of the service they stood up to leave. Suddenly they discovered they were sitting across the aisle from each other. As their eyes met, one man extended his hand to the other and said, "Let's bury the hatchet, Joe. We need to forgive and set our differences behind us. You heard what the pastor said in his sermon." The other extended his hand and agreed. The men subsequently solidified their relationship as they met with me in my office.

The Effects of Preaching

If preaching is so powerful that it can be the means of reconciling two feuding men, it can also heal congregations. Peter Eldersveld, former radio minister of the "Back-to-God Hour," wrote,

Let us not forget that every sermon we preach leaves its mark upon those who hear it, for better or for worse. They are never the same again after hearing it. Even if they turn away they are only proving the point, for that is already a very definite reaction. No, it is not presumptuous for a preacher to say that, for true preaching is the most powerful form of communication in all the world; not because of the preacher, nor because of the sermon itself, but because, if it's a real sermon, it is the voice of the Spirit of God, no matter what the cynics of our day think about it. Even cynics are affected and converted by it.[2]

There is ample data to substantiate this claim. The three thousand converted at Pentecost heard a sermon and were changed. Paul's "sermon" to the Corinthians produced repentance and healing.[3]

Even if I caused you sorrow by my letter, I do not regret it. Though I did regret it—I see that my letter hurt you, but only for a little while—yet now I am happy, not because you were made sorry, but because your sorrow led you to repentance (2 Cor. 7:8–9).

The Bible itself says of the Word preached, "sharper than any double-edged sword, it penetrates even to dividing soul and spirit, joints and marrow; it judges the thoughts and attitudes of the heart" (Heb. 4:12).

Then there are the modern-day examples. Evangelist Billy Graham preaches to huge crowds, many of whom are moved to make decisions for Christ. Radio and television preachers report changes in people through their preaching. Missionaries proclaim the good news, and thousands turn to Christ. Who can deny that preaching changes people's behavior? It is not the power of oratory or the persuasiveness of speech that changes people (1 Cor. 2:1), but the power of the Word preached in the context of grace.

I knew a man who was not a great preacher. Charlie's oratorical skills left something to be desired. What Charlie did when he preached, however, was to expound in simple language what God says in his Word. He had a way of bringing people face-to-face with God. As one parishioner described it: "You always met God in his sermons." Charlie had a way of hiding himself as God spoke to people through his preaching. Charlie's church grew and overcame some internal quibbling because people heard God's Word. One person said, "The preaching may be thin and mediocre, the programs of the church unexciting, but when I hear a word from God, I am fed." Charlie held God up before the people, and that produced change in his church.

Of course, not all preaching has a healing effect. When Paul wrote to Timothy he warned him not to quarrel about words. The preaching of Hymenaeus and Philetus had a gangrenous effect on people (2 Tim. 2:16–18). I know a preacher who is wrecking his church through his preaching because of what he preaches and the way he does it. A church is healed only through the right kind of preaching.

But what is the right kind of preaching? Preaching is proclamation. It may include instructions, counsel, and advice, but it is essentially proclaiming God's will. In preaching, our task is to make God's will for handling and working through a conflict clear to his people. They need to know what God has to say about this conflict, not what everyone else thinks about it. The Word is essential to resolving any conflict, and it is this Word we must preach.

Perhaps there is a small power group that insists on implementing its ideas. They do not like the type of music played by the organist. They complain to the worship committee, send letters to the pastor, and talk among the members about the "terrible music" being played. The governing body of the church has taken a stand on the issue, but this group persists in demanding a different musical menu. Preaching the will of God now becomes important. Preach on doing all things "in a fitting and orderly way" from 1 Corinthians 14:40 or from Philippians 2:1–4, stressing the importance of humility and selflessness. Conflicts are contained and resolved through such preaching, rightly done.

2

Should You Preach?

Before preaching can be done rightly, the preacher needs to be right before God. We cannot evaluate others with God's Word without first honestly, humbly evaluating ourselves before God.

It is imperative that a preacher examine his own heart before God prior to uttering a word to his congregation. If not rightly motivated, his sermons can infect his wounded church. This chapter is an inventory of the pastor's characteristics prerequisite to preaching for recovery. Without these, the pastor can ruin his church.

George began his ministry in a small church in a farming community of Iowa. Usually a new minister tries to please people, but George found himself in deep trouble after two years. It seems that George took offense to any constructive criticism from his parishioners. He was defensive and lectured his parishioners about their faults. It was apparent that any suggestion made to George found its way into next Sunday's sermon by way of rebuttal. These conditions were the makings of a strife-torn church, and after four years George was dismissed.

The scenario was repeated in George's next charge. At this writing he is in his third pastorate, and antagonism is already building.

Unfortunately George is not alone. Many pastors suffer

from personal spiritual myopia. My survey of clergy and church leaders gives evidence that ministerial incompetence is perceived to be the major cause of division.[1] Areas of ineptitude cover a wide range of duties including preaching, administration, counseling, and pastoral work.

A pastor needs to ask, Am I the cause of tension or its solution? Do I produce conflict or dispel it? Often this is difficult to ascertain, because our deceitful hearts can blind us to our own sins. But then we can ask, Do I possess the qualities necessary for effective preaching? What are the qualities needed? We can draw up our own lists, but I find Paul a good model to follow.

Let us set the scene first. The Corinthian church was in deep conflict. It was full of dissension. One group said, "I follow Paul"; another shouted, "I am of Apollos"; others claimed to be disciples of Cephas—or, the more pious, of Christ. These groups all quarreled among themselves (1 Cor. 1:11).

Dissension was also evidenced by lawsuits. Church members were dragging other members to court at the slightest provocation (1 Cor. 6:1). These suits destroyed not only the witness of the church, but also its unity. Church members no longer spoke to one another.

In addition, some people impressed others as elitist. Being "puffed up," they thought themselves "broad-minded," "liberated," "free." They flaunted their "superior strength" before members with a sensitive conscience, creating friction and ill will (1 Cor. 8). Pride produced church conflict.

Like a growing cancer, conflict spread into all areas of Corinthian church life. Selfishness appeared at the Lord's Supper (1 Cor. 11:17–22), chaos emerged in worship (1 Cor. 14:26–33), and the validity of Paul's apostleship was questioned (1 Cor. 9).

Now let's look at Paul. He addressed this church in a sermonic letter. Consider the qualities Paul possessed that made his letter effective.

Humility

Paul exhibited a key quality when he reminded the Corinthian church of the spirit in which he came to them:

> When I came to you, brothers, I did not come with eloquence or superior wisdom as I proclaimed to you the testimony about God. . . . I came to you in weakness and fear, and with much trembling (1 Cor. 2:1, 3).

Paul approached this wounded church from a position of personal weakness, not strength. He was not self-righteous and proud. His words, therefore, were not bombastic and pompous, though they were strong. The people of our congregations will see godliness in us if they see humility. Exemplifying humility is essential to preaching for recovery.

Even if we all agree with this premise, we confront the next question, How do we gauge our humility? Joe Dempsy, a conflict consultant in the Presbyterian Church (U.S.A.), says one of the causes of trauma is the pastor's "inability to absorb criticism." George's pride precluded him from accepting and dealing with criticism. He failed to analyze objectively the validity of criticism or to determine the extent to which it applied to him. If he were to graciously accept parishioners' suggestions for what they were worth, he need not be threatened. Humility is "thinking of yourself with sober judgment" (Rom. 12:3). To judge our humility, we must ask ourselves questions like the following:

Do I know my strengths and weaknesses?

Do I preach from an attitude of humility or superiority?

Is my ego easily bruised, and how do I respond when it is?

Am I usually defensive in my reactions to criticism?

My plane landed at Phoenix International Airport. A former parishioner met me at the gate and spent forty-five minutes with me before my next flight. The conversation turned immediately to his church. I asked him how things were going. I had understood that the church had two ministers, so I inquired who they might be. "Oh," my friend said, "we have one minister now. You see, our minister can't tolerate the competition of another minister in the church." I detected pain and sadness in his voice as he spoke these words.

What is our leadership style? Are we shepherds or generals? Do we know and practice the spirit of foot washing as Jesus instructed us? Do we count ourselves as of no account and others as better than ourselves (Phil. 2:1–8)? Do we display deep sorrow for the conflict and dependence on God for the solution? Do people perceive us as humble, godly leaders? We must think it over before we attempt to serve a church in conflict.

Faithfulness

Ministerial unfaithfulness cuts deeply into the church. We all felt the pain as national media exposed adulterous relationships of popular ministers in 1987 and 1988. Congregations are severely wounded by moral lapses. Adultery, theft, unpaid bills, income tax evasion, and homosexual behavior are sins of unfaithfulness that have been committed by ministers. To preach in a church demands moral faithfulness.

We need to be faithful in our work as pastor. Paul speaks of this: "Now it is required that those who have been given a trust must prove faithful" (1 Cor. 4:2). That trust is first of all the gospel that we must faithfully proclaim (2 Tim. 2:15), but also God's people whom we must faithfully serve (1 Peter 5:1–3). We must have a sense of faithfulness within. Paul says, "My conscience is clear" (1 Cor. 4:4).

Let's take this a step further. What if we betray the Lord and our congregation in a significant way? How can we show fealty to the Lord after breaking our pastoral vows?

A colleague of mine was unfaithful to his wife and had an adulterous relationship with a woman whom he counseled. When the congregation found out, they were obviously disappointed, confused, and discouraged. How could he help heal the church he had wounded?

My friend repented and confessed his sin (Pss. 32; 51).

This brought a measure of healing. The church he served saw "godly sorrow" (2 Cor. 7:10), deep regret, and a humble spirit. Clear devotion to God, unswerving loyalty to Christ, and open admission of guilt continued the healing. Where this is lacking, healing cannot and does not occur.

Servanthood

One common temptation ministers face is a desire for power. This problem becomes acute in churches where the polity of the church places the greatest authority in the minister. Free-lance ministries, churches built by an individual minister, and independent congregations are more susceptible to autocratic, dictatorial operation than churches with strong boards and denominational affiliation. Where jealousy and competition exist, leadership comes to be interpreted as having the power to run a church much as a general commands an army. A retired minister said, "A minister must be a shepherd, not a general. He must lead and serve the sheep, not drive them."

The metaphor is apt. Consider two examples of driving God's flock instead of serving it. A minister recently came to serve a church in southern California. He took over the finances, ran the church into bankruptcy, and left with a pocketful of money. A minister in Colorado dreamed of building a superchurch. By continually borrowing money he built a three-million-dollar facility and began many ministries. But he neglected his flock. The church splintered and ended in bankruptcy.

Neither of these pastors knew how to be God's servant to his people. What about you? You may be a great organizer, an adroit businessman, and a clever financier, but are you a servant? When you begin to preach in a church in conflict, you must understand the hurts, pain, needs, and suffering of the people. You must mount the pulpit, not with a bat or club to wound, but with a basin of water to wash swollen and aching feet. Jesus taught his disciples this approach (John 13:15), and Paul echoed the same spirit when he wrote, "So

then, men ought to regard us as servants of Christ" (1 Cor.
4:1) and "What, after all, is Apollos? And what is Paul? Only
servants through whom you came to believe, as the Lord has
assigned to each his task" (1 Cor. 3:5). By serving the
congregation, one serves Christ.

A servant-shepherd is a person whose life is reasonably
integrated so that he does not have to spend a lot of time
working out his own agenda and problems through the
church. If a pastor only serves his own needs, disaster ensues
for his people.

Pastor Smith has come to a stable, traditional church in a
large city. The neighborhood was at one time homogeneous
and all the members lived near the church. Younger members,
however, began moving to the suburbs but kept attending
out of loyalty and family ties. The prospect of losing those
members to more convenient suburban churches bothered
Pastor Smith, since his ambition was to make his church a
superchurch. He changed the style of worship and introduced
new, "exciting" programs. To meet the population trends he
brought a progressive mentality into leadership and weeded
out stubborn resistant members. A new blueprint for ministry
was adopted. But this vision for the church was not the
congregation's vision. It was a vision tied to Pastor Smith's
self-concept. He wanted to prove himself successful. He
pushed his agenda until he succeeded, but he left a trail of
hurt, wounded, and bleeding sheep. He was working to
satisfy his own ego. He was most obviously not a servant-
shepherd.

This problem is further complicated when a pastor is
unaware that he has a personal agenda. He may perceive his
plan as God's will for the church, a glorious vision of what
God wants for this congregation. As Harold Pierce of the
Southern Baptist Convention said, "Pastors often have a sense
of need for power to feel secure."[2]

A servant-shepherd is secure in Christ and is willing to
give himself to others. He is more interested in Christ's sheep
than himself. He is at peace with himself and does not have to

"prove" his abilities and worth. Personal success, being liked by everyone, and admired by peers are not priorities. His goal is to serve Christ and his church selflessly. He listens, then asks, "What is the agenda of this church? What do they want to happen? What are their needs? What does Christ expect?" This does not mean that the pastor of a strife-torn congregation must be free from personal problems; it means he must center his preaching around the needs of the church and not his own. In fact, his own problems, rightly handled, can make him more understanding and empathetic toward the congregation. Experiencing disappointment, rejection, and alienation should bring an authenticity to his preaching.

If you plan to serve a battered church, be ready to be a servant who must perform the most menial task, listen to many hurts, suffer with the disillusioned, and be patient with the angry. I have often felt like a pincushion, stabbed by the reactions of people to church fights.

Self-Sacrifice

Recovery is the first goal of the minister in a strife-torn church. But recovery doesn't mean implementing our own agenda. This is the first sacrifice a minister must make. We may think the church needs new programs, new buildings, new activities, but it first needs healing. We need to quiet all our ideas to hear the anguished cries of the church. They will want to tell us the story of their trauma. Each story will differ from the other as it is perceived by various people. We may hear this story *ad nauseam*. Even our privacy at times may be invaded by those who want to talk about the terrible trauma in the church.

Paul addressed this issue in the Corinthian letter. He spoke of rights that he refused to exercise so that the Corinthian church might be healed. He was wholly self-sacrificing; he refused to impose personal needs on the church so that his teachings would be accepted (1 Cor. 9:4–6, 15). The cause of Christ in the lives of these people was Paul's primary concern.

As pastors we must communicate a readiness to give, to sacrifice, to go to any length to heal the wounds of the church. This must be our goal. This is why we have come to the church. We must serve—just like our Master (Luke 22:27). Christ's entire ministry demonstrated such self-sacrifice.

Are we ready to walk the second mile with joy? Will we take the time to listen, to feel the hurts, to shed tears with our troubled people? Will we with Moses say, "Bring me any case too hard for you, and I will hear it" (Deut. 1:17)? We must be ready to imitate God himself, who carried Israel "on eagles' wings" (Ex. 19:4). Our preaching in a strife-torn church will be relevant and penetrating as the people observe our self-sacrificing spirit.

Other Qualities

There are other qualities we need to minister to a hurting church. We should have an extraordinary amount of love, genuine *agape* love. Consider the love Paul demonstrated toward the churches. "I have worked much harder, been in prison more frequently, been flogged more severely, and been exposed to death again and again" (2 Cor. 11:23). Paul's love was sacrificial to the point of being painful. True love seeks the highest welfare of the object of love. When a congregation perceives this in us, the setting is ripe for healing. After a confrontational sermon, a parishioner said to me, "Pastor, you go the second mile; we know you love us." I have on occasion literally told my people, "I love you dearly," because I knew they needed that assurance.

We need to be especially compassionate, sympathetic, and empathetic, not easily irritated, impulsive, or headstrong. We also need patience, vision, sincerity, enthusiasm, courage, and moral stamina. Facing the winds and crosscurrents of conflict demands a strong commitment to this type of ministry. We will be buffeted about and challenged at the crucial junctions where people's feelings run high. Managing conflict is hard work. Preaching to a congregation embroiled in conflict is even more demanding. We, more than anyone else, must be calm in the raging storm.

Are we up to the task? This is not only a spiritual consideration. We have to take a good look at our physical health. People with heart disease and high blood pressure are not likely to be strong enough to help a strife-torn church. H. Beecher Hicks, Jr., writes,

> Do not underestimate the pervasive power of the storm. Its effect can be devastating to mind and body. During this onslaught my physical stamina waned and I found myself hospitalized with a dangerous case of high blood pressure. Preaching through a storm requires of us vigilance in body, mind, soul, and spirit. It is in this way we love our Lord best.[3]

So it's clear that much needs to be considered seriously before a person can preach for recovery. Words alone are not enough. James Stalker wrote,

> We are so constituted that what we hear depends very much for its effect on how we are disposed towards him who speaks. The regular hearers of a minister gradually form in their minds, almost unaware, an image of what he is into which they put everything which they themselves remember about him and everything which they have heard of his record; and, when he rises on Sunday in the pulpit, it is not the man visible there at the moment that they listen to, but his image, which stands behind him and determines the precise weight and effect of every sentence which he utters.[4]

Although it is God who heals a divided church, the earthly vessel he uses is vital. God trained Moses many years. He set aside Paul for preparation. Jesus provided a model for his disciples so they might be fit for God's use. Perhaps God is calling you to preach in a strife-torn church. Perhaps not. If you have not yet developed the qualities mentioned in this chapter, you might well add trauma to a church instead of reducing it.

Because some ministers are especially vulnerable to

conflict, they leave a trail of torn churches behind them. These pastors have a propensity to produce tension and polarize people. The prerequisite for pastors who are able to heal a congregation through preaching can be summarized in Paul's words to the Thessalonian church:

> You are witnesses, and so is God, of how holy, righteous, and blameless we were among you who believed. For you know that we dealt with each of you as a father deals with his own children, encouraging, comforting and urging you to live lives worthy of God, who calls you into his kingdom and glory (1 Thess. 2:10–12).

3

Spirit-Powered Preaching

I am totally opposed to moving the church from this location," Jake announced. "We have been on this corner for sixty-five years and I see no reason why we should move. This building has served us well. It has character, class, and ample room for our congregation to worship. Besides, moving will cost a lot of money. Think of what it will do to the old people living in this area."

Jake went on, citing myriad arguments for not relocating. He had a sizable following who agreed. At the last membership meeting, fifty-two percent had voted not to relocate.

The affluent people in the congregation, however, wanted a new facility. The nursery was obsolete, there was no parking lot, the educational facilities were woefully inadequate. There was some justification for a new church.

The congregation was deadlocked. Year after year the impasse remained. Both sides were becoming bitter, angry, and often hateful toward each other.

Imagine that you are the newly arrived pastor. What message would you bring? What kind of preaching would calm the congregation, clarify the salient issues, and cultivate harmony and direction?

Paul's approach to a similar situation was to inform the church that his preaching was a "demonstration of the Spirit's power" (1 Cor. 2:4). In Paul's letter this wounded and divided congregation heard a Spirit-powered message. Rather than addressing the Corinthian church with "wise and persuasive words," Paul sent a message given by the Spirit. This is central to the authority of Paul's words. How can we give a message from the Holy Spirit?

The Greeks of Corinth liked rational, philosophical, logical preaching. But Paul knew such preaching would not solve problems at Corinth; nor will it solve ours. We may give logical arguments, persuasive words, and rational reasons to convince our congregations not to fight about the relocation, but it will do little good. What our people need is the Holy Spirit's message. Spirit-powered preaching is preaching the Word the Holy Spirit gave us. The content of our message must be the Spirit-inspired Word of God.

The Content of Preaching

Our task, then, in a situation like Jake's is to determine what passages of Scripture have a bearing on the relocation controversy. To do this well, we can further examine what factors in this fight are addressed in Scripture. The particulars of any conflict are not necessarily addressed in Scripture specifically. Yet the underpinnings of the fight are considered there. What are the attitudes perpetuating this conflict? What are the motivations? What goal is the congregation striving to attain? These elements of the conflict are just as real as the surface issues. It is to these kinds of issues that the Holy Spirit speaks.

Let us consider the specific example of Jake's church. What could help resolve the conflict? We might begin with a series of sermons from the book of Nehemiah. I once preached from this book with great profit, with the following sermon themes:

"Seeing Broken Walls"	Neh. 1
"Plan Ahead"	Neh. 2
"Facing the Critics"	Neh. 4
"What Are Your Hang-Ups?"	Neh. 5

"A Spiritual Retreat"	Neh. 8:9–12
"Renewal"	Neh. 9–10
"Total Dedication"	Neh. 11:1–2; 12:27, 43
"Effective Christian Service"	Neh. 13

These titles suggest that a number of issues involving the relocation of a church can be confronted through preaching. For example, we can present the need to rebuild the church. Who are the real enemies in this conflict? Should we battle each other or the spiritual forces mentioned in Ephesians 6? Couple these sermons with a spiritual renewal conference or a retreat to bring the people together in unity. Give them a vision of what can be done if they work together. All this and more can be found in this Scripture. Using the appropriate Scripture as the basis of our preaching will enable the people to hear what the Spirit is saying to the church (Rev. 2–3).

If there is a wrong attitude in the church, preach on Philippians 2:2–4:

> Make my joy complete by being like-minded, having the same love, being one in spirit and purpose. Do nothing out of selfish ambition or vain conceit, but in humility consider others better than yourselves. Each of you should look not only to your own interests, but also to the interests of others.

How can anyone insist on his own way in a relocation controversy if this passage is personally applied? Preach boldly what the Spirit has given you to preach.

Another facet of this issue is determining what the Spirit says about the purpose and calling of the church. Does one location fulfill that purpose better than another? Is there a need to evangelize in the church's present community? Are we abandoning an inner city area of need? Will the church be able to reach out more effectively at a new location?

And what does the Spirit say about stewardship? Sermons on this subject will enable people to compare the costs of relocation and the costs of remaining.

Preach on the basic principles that enter into the decision

and ask God's Spirit to demonstrate his power to heal. Show from Scripture that the way members of the congregation conduct themselves in the conflict is more important than the outcome.

What is *our* agenda? We may be tempted to preach according to "human wisdom" (1 Cor. 2:4–5). We may even look at the situation and decide to take sides. Will we preach our opinions and justify our position, or will we allow the principles of Scripture to bear on the issues?

Perhaps we may even fear preaching about the conflict and be tempted to ignore it altogether. If so, we need to ask whether God has a word from the Holy Spirit for this broken congregation. If so, how can we fail to speak it?

The Form of the Message

Pastor Carl was visibly angry. He was disgusted with all the bickering in his church. People were at each other's throats; the unity of the church was dissipating like a morning fog. Carl's frustration was showing in his sermons. There was cynicism, hardness, and censoriousness. His words were biting; they cut like a razor.

One Sunday Carl preached a sermon on forgiveness based on Matthew 18:35: "This is how my heavenly Father will treat each of you unless you forgive your brother from the heart." His interpretation of the passage was correct, but as he preached he used blistering words, lambasting, castigating, condemning, and scolding his people. Some said afterward that "he lost his cool." Others went home guilt-laden and ashamed. A few were angry and demanded an apology. Was Pastor Carl right? Should he have preached differently? Or was this Spirit-powered preaching?

The issue here is whether Carl's preaching had the earmarks of the Spirit. Those distinguishing marks are the fruit of the Spirit: love, kindness, gentleness, self-control, patience, compassion, honesty, and integrity—to mention a few (see Galatians 5:22–23). Carl obviously was carried away with his emotions and did not demonstrate these qualities.

Just as a child quickly feels the mood of a parent, a congregation easily senses the disposition of its pastor.

So now the focus is on us as preachers. Every time we approach the pulpit in a strife-torn church, we need to ask, Do I love these people? Do I understand their trauma? Am I as compassionate and patient as my Savior?

Only once is it recorded that Jesus was angry, the result of the Jewish leaders' being more concerned about their laws than about a man with a shriveled hand. "He looked around at them in anger, and deeply distressed at their stubborn hearts, said to the man, 'Stretch out your hand'" (Mark 3:5). Yet even then, Jesus was "deeply distressed"—not vindictive. The congregation will quickly sense whether our approach is tempered by the Holy Spirit or by our feelings.

Do we preach down to the people from an attitude of superiority? Is our honor at stake, or the honor of Christ? Do we find ourselves defending our actions and words? Do we have a paranoiac stance? Do we project hopelessness, despair, and fatalism? Do we find ourselves being blunt, slashing out at people, demanding they shape up?

Preaching can only heal "with a demonstration of the Spirit's power" (1 Cor. 2:4). This means that words of admonition are given with a sense of pain. Some things need to be said in a whisper, a gentle tone of voice, out of an agonizing heart. Effective healing takes place when we preach grace and the people sense that we have experienced a good measure of it. We should let our preaching demonstrate the Spirit's power as God shapes us into godly, obedient servants. Our people can easily tell if we are living with and under the power of the Spirit.

The Holy Spirit, Preaching, and Change

Once I cut my hand. The gash was deep, producing a flow of blood. After washing the wound, I placed a Band-Aid on it that had to be replaced several hours later. In a couple of days, a scab had formed, so I dispensed with the Band-Aid. Imperceptibly, healing took place over the next two weeks.

The wound became smaller until finally the scab fell off, leaving a beautifully healed scar. I do not know the process that took place under the scab, but my body had the capacity to knit the torn flesh together.

In just such an invisible, gradual way the Holy Spirit heals a church. In my own case I cannot say exactly when the church was healed. Was it when we decided to add a second staff person? Was it when we agreed to remodel the church? Had we arrived when we celebrated our seventy-fifth anniversary? Slowly, mysteriously, the Spirit was bringing us together in fellowship. The healing of a church is a process through which the Holy Spirit produces change.

The Spirit is God's change agent. Out of the basic, radical change of rebirth (John 3:5–8; 2 Cor. 5:17) come many other changes as the Spirit renews, revives, and restores (1 Peter 1:2). Ultimately the healing of a church is the work of the Holy Spirit, changing people's attitudes and restoring relationships.

The Spirit does not work in a vacuum. Changes occur where people experience God's love and love for each other. This is where we need to examine our preaching closely. Is our preaching seasoned with grace? Do people receive a message that not only points out weaknesses, but also concentrates on the grace of God? Do they hear "good news" or "bad news"? It is essential that our preaching create a climate for the Holy Spirit to do his work of healing.

I have observed the following traits in people involved in conflict: "Hatred, discord, jealousy, fits of rage, selfish ambition, dissensions, factions and envy" (Gal. 5:20). Paul describes these as acts of the sinful nature. The problem is that people with these traits are not living by the Spirit. Such an atmosphere is not used by the Spirit to heal the wounds of conflict. Our preaching can change that. Preaching can create an entirely new environment that God will use to heal the church. This preaching must strongly emphasize what God has done for them in Christ. Stress the centrality of the cross, the sacrifice of Christ, the unconditional love of God. Open the Scriptures and reveal the mighty works of God. Paul invariably stressed the work of God before he told his readers how they should act. The indicative must always precede the imperative.

This is not just true for our congregations. We need to concentrate on the scope of God's love and power for us ourselves. Looking at Jesus gives strength to persevere in the difficult circumstances.

Is our preaching Spirit-powered? Strife-torn churches desperately need to hear what the Spirit says. They need to see us as Spirit-filled, Spirit-controlled, Spirit-led ministers. Not only what we say, but how we say it will demonstrate whether our preaching is Spirit-powered.

If we have the qualifications identified in chapter 2 and we are a Spirit-empowered person in our preaching, we can be shepherds whom God can use to heal broken churches. Next we must learn how to heal broken relationships through preaching. That is the subject of the next chapter.

4

Relational Preaching

Rocky Mountain News recently carried a story about a minister who isn't evangelistic enough for some in his congregation.[1] Apparently he was suing eight church members for defaming him and trying to get him fired. The lawsuit charged that four couples had "instituted a campaign of letter-writing, telephone calls, and personal verbal attacks" in an effort to force his resignation. The couples were accused of spreading rumors and whispering and making faces while the minister preached.

The pastor requested a hearing before a district judge to prohibit the couples from attending services. The judge refused on the grounds that he could not put a restraint on the free exercise of speech or religion.

What was the result of this hostility? One church member said the dispute has caused a serious rift in the congregation. This is a clear example of broken relationships that desperately need healing.

Broken Relationships

How can frayed relationships in a congregation be restored? How can families where there is alienation between parent and child, brother and sister be reunited? Suppose our congregation has people who do not speak to one another, who ignore each other, gossip, and spread rumors about each other. Perhaps they are downright nasty and mean! What will we do to mend these fractures? What ointment will we pour on the festering sores?

Perhaps you wonder whether our preaching can play a significant role in recovery. The contention of this book is that it can—and must! Begin by preaching on relationships.

"As I see it, trauma is not generally, certainly not primarily, caused by theological/social issues, but interpersonal relationships (e.g., ministers and congregation or council members)." That is the way a pastor in Stockton, California, sees the situation. "I believe that most problems in our churches have to do with staff relations, people to people relations. Doctrine is sometimes used as an excuse to avoid the people issue."[2] Time and again pastors have told me that healing comes through the restoration of relationships.

I do not propose a dichotomy between relational preaching and doctrinal preaching. Each informs the other. Nor am I arguing for relational preaching as the exclusive approach to preaching in a divided church. But preaching on relationships plays an important role in the recovery process and ought to be consciously pursued. To achieve this involves dealing with at least three vital areas: a person's relationship to God, to others, and to himself.

Building Relationships

The Vertical Relationship

Jack and Sally were struggling in their devotional life. Although at one time they were very active members of the church, their interest had begun to wane. They no longer volunteered for ministries. They became more critical, irritated, and upset by contention in the church. Worst of all, their prayer life suffered. They felt as if God was far from them. They had no desire to pray, and they could not understand how God could allow so much bloodletting in the church.

There are many Jacks and Sallys with lives caught in the

web of church strife. Ironically, the strife is often both the cause and the result of a broken relationship with God.

A congregation's most basic relationship is the one they have with God. When this connection is severed or damaged, fights and quarrels result:

> What causes fights and quarrels among you? Don't they come from your desires that battle within you? You want something but don't get it. You kill and covet, but you cannot have what you want. You quarrel and fight. You do not have, because you do not ask God. When you ask, you do not receive, because you ask with wrong motives, that you may spend what you get on your pleasures (James 4:1–3).

The real causes of conflict lie within each person. Yet the battle is not intrapsychic, but spiritual. It has to do with one's basic allegiance. The Lord God is no longer the aim and focus of love and loyalty. Rather, the goal becomes winning the fight and getting one's way.

Church fights also result in a retrenchment of a person's relationship to God. Spiritual life does not flourish. The acts of the sinful nature become obvious: "fits of rage, selfish ambition, dissensions, factions and envy" (Gal. 5:20). These undercut life in the Spirit.

How will we begin restoring this relationship with God through preaching? First, the people need to be instructed on how to be right with God. This involves preaching about confession, repentance, and forgiveness. With David, our parishioners must say, "Against you, you only, have I sinned and done what is evil in your sight" (Ps. 51:4). This is where healing starts. The people must know that strife is odious to God. As long as there is no acknowledgment of wrong, no sorrow for the terrible rift in the church, no desire for forgiveness from God, there will be little healing. It is true of a church as it was true in Israel:

> If my people, who are called by my name, will humble themselves and pray and seek my face and turn from their

wicked ways, then I will hear from heaven and will forgive
their sin and will heal their land (2 Chron. 7:14).

God heals his church, too, only through humility, prayer, and
repentance.

Second, preach grace. Lead the people to the cross of
Calvary where they can lay down pride, hurts, and demands.
Give them heavy doses of the heady new wine of God's love
and mercy. Preach sermons that stress what God has done for
them in Christ. Show them both the holiness and the love of
God. Lead them through preaching to a close and intimate
walk with God.

Third, preach about prayer. The solution to fights and
quarrels is simple: pray. James tells us that people do not have
because they do not ask (James 4:2). Show the necessity,
practice, and blessings of prayer. Urge them to establish
prayer groups and come to prayer meetings.

Suppose that Jack and Sally hear us preach on prayer and
decide they must begin praying about their own relationship
with God. As they confess the terrible hurt of the poisoning
fray in their church, God begins the healing process. No one
calls on God in vain (Matt. 7:7–11). Confession itself has
great healing power. Now that they have reestablished
contact with God, they can go on to build relationships with
others and themselves.

The Horizontal Relationships

God

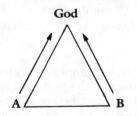

A   **B**

This figure illustrates what happens when two people or
parties restore their relationship with God. As A and B move
closer to God, they move closer to each other.

As Jack and Sally develop their walk with God, they will

want to rebuild relationships with others. Perhaps they will begin attending a small growth group or prayer cell. In response to preaching, people may begin to open up and confess hostile feelings to God, thus releasing bottled-up emotions of love. You may think this is impossible, but in 1 Corinthians 13 the apostle Paul told his divided church how they were to treat each other, thereby releasing a strong ·current of love. I used this chapter as the basis for a series of sermons shortly after beginning to serve a strife-torn church. People indicated they found it helpful because it taught them how to begin to love one another.

People in a church squabble can be miserable, unattractive, mean, and unfair. Our first reaction may be to despise or reject them. Those in the fracas may desire revenge. How can we get people to love one another? Through preaching on relationships.

Here is a sample sermon based on 1 Corinthians 13:4. My first sermon in this series had as its text the first four verses of this chapter and was entitled "The Supremacy of Love." The sermon contrasted love with the other gifts mentioned such as tongues, prophecy, faith, and giving. This second sermon deals with the character of love as patient and kind.

*   *   *

Sermon: "Love Is Patient and Kind"

Scripture Reading: 1 Corinthians 13
Text: 1 Corinthians 13:4a, "Love is patient, love is kind."

Dear friends in Christ,

What is the best way to improve, correct, and strengthen the life of this church? How can the problems of tension, schism, and anger be solved? According to the apostle Paul, the most excellent way is the way of love.

The greatest gift to the church is not the gift of tongues, or prophecy, or faith, or self-sacrifice. It is love. In fact, to possess these gifts and not have love adds up to one big zero. Love comes to expression in patience and kindness.

I. God Wants You to Be Patient

People often say to me, "Pastor, I wish I had more patience. I seem to be so impatient with my family, with other people, and those close to me." They remind me of the person who prayed, "Lord, give me patience, and give it to me now!"

Patience in the New Testament is not resignation or blind submission. It is not "grinning and bearing." The two words used in the New Testament for patience literally mean "to be long in spirit" or "to stay put, to endure." Patience is not a passive yielding but an active enduring.

For example, I know a young man who wanted to be a doctor. He studied hard to accomplish his goal. In spite of his diligence, his G.P.A. was not high enough for acceptance into medical school. He also ran out of money. It seemed he should give up his ambition and seek another vocation. Instead he found a job in a hospital, worked to save money, took classes at night, and trained himself in preparation for medical school. Finally he joined the Air Force and was admitted to a school of medicine. Today he is a practicing physician. He had patience! Patient people endure, don't give up. In relationships with others, patient people are long in spirit.

Patience means having a long fuse. Some people have short fuses that easily ignite. Patient persons have long ones. Are you a patient person? In your relationships with others, are you long in spirit?

In Corinth, people were irritating each other. They were hurting each other with cutting, unkind remarks. They had little tolerance. Life was becoming more miserable each day. You know what that's like, don't you! Other people easily aggravate and offend you. Perhaps you are disgusted and downright angry about what is happening in the church. You feel it is time to jump into the fray and slash with your sword to get even and retaliate! After all, this must stop! Right now!

God's message to you is "love is patient." You must learn patience. James writes, "Be patient, then, brothers, until the Lord's coming" (James 5:7). He then gives three illustrations of patience.

The first is the farmer who waits for the land to yield its crop. He waits for the spring to come, the time for seeding, the rains, the appearance of the tiny sprout, the growth of the plant, the kernel, the ripening of the kernel, and finally the harvest. If he wants to enjoy the fruits of harvest, he must endure the warm spring and hot summer. Have you learned this kind of patience? No? Well, you live in the Now Generation, the instant economy. No wonder! A generation with little understanding of true love. But love knows how to wait—how to wait for the healing of our church through building fellowship with each other.

James's second illustration is that of the prophets. They are "an example of patience in the face of suffering" (James 5:10). Although abused, accused, maligned, persecuted, and blamed for hard times, they were long-fused. Think of Moses or Jeremiah. They persevered while suffering abuse. Think of Jesus, who was patient in his suffering. We too are a suffering church. There is enough blame for everyone. In all this we must learn to be patient, because love involves patience with others.

James's third illustration is Job. "You have heard of Job's perseverance" (James 5:11). If anyone was pelted with troubles, it was Job. Bereft of his property and children, misunderstood by his friends, accused by his wife, he endured; he was long-fused. Patience is not stoic silence or a fatalistic attitude toward troubles. Patience involves great struggle, but in the struggle love perseveres. Love is patient. It endures.

To become more patient, you need to look to God, the paradigm of patience. If anyone has reason to be impatient, to be short-fused, to throw up his hands in despair, to be disgusted and irritated, it is God. He has to face rebellious, wayward, disobedient people all the time. A few times it became so serious, he almost gave up. Once he said, "I will wipe mankind . . . from the face of the earth" (Gen. 6:7). Israel too gave God much pain and agony in times of apostasy. But God never gave up! His patient love kept him from destroying the earth. He took a positive stance toward it. Even by destroying the wicked, he was in reality saving the earth. God is not short-fused. He takes the long view. His program of redemption slowly unfolded through the ages and culminated in the birth, death, and resurrection of Christ. You need to learn from God above all; if God can be so patient with you, you ought to be patient with each other.

Christ exhibited great patience. It was supremely demonstrated when he "endured such opposition from sinful men" (Heb. 12:3). The cross stands as the greatest monument to patient endurance. There he patiently suffered God's judgment—for you.

If you are a follower of Christ, he wants to find patience, a fruit of the Spirit, in your life too.

Love is patient. Don't say you love others when you are impatient with them. If you truly love others, you will be patient with them. If an injustice has been done to you, patience enables you to turn the other cheek. Don't be in a rush to get revenge. Keep your verbal sword in its sheath. Love is patient!

II. God Wants You to Be Kind

Patience is the side of love that endures, that is long in spirit. Kindness is the side of love that reaches out to others. It is not enough to endure the rages of some angry person or refrain from revenge. God expects you to treat others kindly.

The highest example of kindness is found in God himself. I think the devil had the surprise of his life when God came down to the garden after Adam and Eve sinned. He must have expected a great explosion of anger with a judgment of eternal expulsion. Instead he saw God searching for his creatures with the question, "Adam, Eve, where are you?" There was a tenderness in his voice. It was the voice of a parent seeking his child. In that act, God was showing grace and kindness. That is the way of love. In response to Satan's "no" to creation—to his desire to destroy it, to bring conflict, trouble, alienation, and death to it—God came with his "yes" of preservation, redemption, restoration, and renewal. "The LORD is good to all; he has compassion on all he has made" (Ps. 145:9). Love is kind.

There is a brand of kindness that people experience in our world that flows from refinement and culture. People are taught to be considerate, polite, courteous. Children are taught to say "thank you," "excuse me," or "I'm sorry." Or we engage in kind remarks such as "that is a beautiful dress you are wearing." Much flattery and sophistication exists in such empty phrases. Often our kindness is dishonest, a sham dripping with hypocrisy.

Genuine, honest kindness flows from love. This kindness is a fruit of the Holy Spirit (Galatians 5:22). The fruit of kindness comes to expression in your life as you "live by the Spirit" and not by your "sinful nature." You must crucify the desire to gossip, produce dissension, promote factions, and even express yourself in fits of rage. You will need to cultivate the fruits of patience and kindness.

Love is both patient and kind. If you love, both patience and kindness will be shown to others. Do you belong to a group that finds itself impatient with others in the church? Is it hard to be kind to others in this congregation? Well, let's change all that. Begin today by thinking of an act of kindness you can show to someone—perhaps someone with whom you have had some differences. It may be a small kindness, but it will lead to greater things. Begin thinking kindly about this person and start to pray for him. Think of the more excellent way. Think of God's way—his patience—his kindness. Remember Christ's patience and kindness to you—who does not deserve it. Resolve now to follow the more excellent way! The way of love![3]

*   *   *

Sermons like "Love Is Patient and Kind" enable people to come to grips with the basic issues underlying the conflict. Problems can be solved when the relationships between people are wholesome and right. Sermons on the "one another" passages of Scripture also help build relationships. It takes time to build bridges, but people begin to change as they are convicted of unbiblical behavior by the preaching of the Word of God. This is how preaching heals a church. This is how my church was healed.

The Inner Relationship

Ungodly behavior that precipitates and perpetuates conflict is always a consequence of a sinful attitude or motivation. The deepening of the Christian's experience of Christ necessarily entails a look inward while relying on God's love. A pastor has a duty to encourage this type of examination by unfolding what the Bible says about the particular sins besetting his church. The following profiles represent some sins commonly seen in churches filled with strife.

Jim is very proud—and very rich. He expects his ideas to be heard, approved, and executed with haste. Jim has caused many quarrels in his church. His problem lies within himself: "Pride only breeds quarrels" (Prov. 13:10). He is deceived by his pride: "The pride of your heart has deceived you" (Obad. 3). Jim neither understands nor correctly assesses his proper place in his church. He does not see his own limitations. Preaching on pride, one of the so-called deadly sins, may awaken Jim (and others) to the need to reexamine his inner life. Invariably pride lies at the heart of church conflicts.

Eva is a totally negative person. She feels she is worthless. She loathes herself, and her size does nothing to mitigate these feelings. It may seem Eva would never create problems; she passively comes and goes without a whimper. But "there is, in fact, an obvious connection between a negative self-image and a critical attitude toward others. The person who is always running other people down is, very likely, trying to bolster his own ego."[4] Eva is doing just that. She is critical of the organist, the secretary, and the staff, and she voices her criticisms at membership meetings. There is little if any praise in her speech.

Churches with many Evas constantly feel threatened until the basic problem is addressed. How do we achieve a proper and healthy self-image? Our preaching must tackle this, even though our patience and persistence will be tried as we deal with our Eva.

Joe, by contrast, has a problem with authority. He attacks all the authority figures in the church: the pastor, the board, associate pastors, teachers, and anyone who holds a responsible position. He argues every proposal we promote. He causes endless arguments and garners others to support his views. He knows how to use parliamentary procedure, the bylaws of our organization, and any other means to humiliate or frustrate us. We must preach to Joe. Though intelligent, witty, and well educated, he is a thorn in the side of our congregation. He will not take advice or counsel. He is a law to himself. What should we say?

We may be inclined to tell Joe to knuckle under to God's authority and that of the elders of the church (Heb. 13:7). But Joe's problem is an inner one. He is proud and arrogant. So we begin by preaching about those things that will help him change. Joe's problem is inside himself, so we have to be patient. We must be long in our love for him. Until Joe sees this he will continue to be a problem in the church.

Jim, Eva, and Joe all need to hear that they are accepted by God through faith in Christ. Don't forget that people are often working out their personal problems through creating conflict in the church. We need to preach with this in mind. We must ask ourselves in the Holy Spirit how we can create healthy attitudes, an atmosphere where people love each other and see themselves as they really are. Pray for God to bring this about. Through the sermons lead them to an understanding of who they are. Show them what to "put off" (Eph. 4:25–32) and what to "put on" (Eph. 4:24).

Rebuilding the house of God—his church—is a slow and painful process. It is a work only accomplished brick by brick by brick. Often each brick is damaged and needs to be remade; so the building of the house takes even longer. The challenge of rebuilding a destroyed congregation is a great one, but it is a worthy job. God can be gloriously honored as we grapple with our congregations to rebuild relationships. We need to concentrate on fostering godly relationships. Though our preaching need not always be relational, a good deal of it should be.

How specific should we be in our preaching? Should we address the conflict issues directly and forthrightly? Is there a correct time to confront from the pulpit? These questions will be considered in the next chapter.

5

Confrontational Preaching

The necessity of confrontation has been established, but this is only the beginning. Now we need to examine closely the most effective ways to confront.

Some people have very structured approaches. I recently met with George O. Fraser, leader of Titus Task Force Ministries. This interim-ministry team enters a strife-torn church to "straighten out what was left unfinished" (Titus 1:5). Fraser related how the team prepares to enter a church and the tasks it assumes upon arriving. There are diagnostic studies, debriefings of the church staff, review of current and past activities, timelines, schedules, and finances to establish and document.

Once the preliminary work is done, Fraser comes with complete authority to do what he believes must be done to heal the body of believers. He compares himself to a surgeon whose patient has a fast-growing cancer: with the authorization document for surgery signed, he excises whatever is necessary. Fraser comes to a church to perform surgery. The patient does not dictate what must be done; it's the other way around.

Fraser's first sermon is a direct confrontation of sin in the congregation. Both personal and corporate sins are named one by one. The leadership are confronted and admonished to confess their responsibility for the conflict. Sins committed by members of the congregation are openly exposed. People are told to think of others they have offended. They are not to ask *whether* they have offended anyone, but *whom* they have offended. Everyone is on a ninety-day probation—the pastor, the council, and individual members. When people leave the worship service they must be mad, glad, or convicted! There is no room for indifference.

Obviously such confrontation is carried on in a tightly controlled and supervised context. There may be occasions when a congregation needs such radical surgery. Fraser considers himself a specialist. Perhaps you see yourself as a general practitioner. Should you attempt such radical confrontation? Will you begin by identifying the sins of your congregation? If so, how will you do this?

Many pastors are not so tightly structured. In my survey I asked ministers in churches this question: "What style of preaching did you find most effective in healing a traumatized church (e.g., teaching, confronting, pastoral, counseling, a combination of these, other)?" Eighty percent responded that they used a combination of styles depending on the occasion. One said, "Definitely a combination of all of these. Any confrontation should be done on a biblical basis in a teaching atmosphere with pastoral counseling to iron out the wrinkles."

But what is the biblical basis for confrontation? Is there a biblical example that provides insight into the needs of our congregation? The apostle Paul appears to have provided such a model when he wrote to the Corinthians.

Know the Facts

Before confronting a congregation, we must collect accurate data. Paul identified his source of information, thereby mitigating questions about his information. He was given information from a reliable source in Corinth: "My brothers, some from Chloe's household have informed me that there are quarrels among you" (1 Cor. 1:11). He also received a letter from the Corinthians asking questions about marriage, Christian liberty, matters pertaining to worship (especially the Lord's Supper), and the use of spiritual gifts (1 Cor. 7:1). Apparently Stephanus, Fortunatus, and Achaicus supplied data about church problems (1 Cor. 16:17). On the basis of this firsthand knowledge Paul was able to respond confrontationally to the trauma. Before we preach a confrontational sermon, we must be sure we know the facts.

A large California church was having problems. No one quite knew the cause, but there were obvious divisions and a lack of direction. A senior pastor and twenty-five staff people headed a number of programs in education, evangelism, youth, music, and women's ministries. Despite this variety of activities, something was wrong, although no one knew why. The church was losing members, people were unhappy, and the worship was dull. After reviewing all aspects of the church, it was discovered that no meaningful communication took place between the members of the staff.[1] To confront this church about unity without recognizing the true cause for disunity would not have brought healing. Know the facts.

My survey indicates that power struggles are the third major cause of trauma. How will we get to the bottom of a power struggle? Only with great patience, wisdom, and discernment. Perhaps a wealthy, long-time, especially vocal member is behind the struggles. Or the governing board may be weak. It may even be that we ourselves are battling for more power.

Getting the facts entails much probing, listening, reading, and talking. Consult those who know the congregation, dig into its history, pinpoint the heart of the issue. Judge the depth and emotional levels of the conflict so you can confront effectively. Preach from facts, not fiction.

Establish Trust

We may be tempted to preach on the sins of the congregation as soon as we see them. But don't be hasty in confronting the church with specific sins. I spent ten years in a church before confronting them on a specific issue of respect, submission, and obedience to God's lawful authorities in the church.[2] They were showing a sinful attitude in a specific action, and I confronted them on that issue. But my confrontation was rooted in years of loving service to this congregation. There was a reservoir of trust. After the confrontation one person said, "You had the right to say what you did and we know you said it because you love us. It must have been difficult for you." You may not have to wait ten years, but confrontation is only redemptive in the context of a loving, caring relationship.

Paul was able to confront the Corinthian church because he had established a relationship of trust. He was their first pastor, the founder of the church. They were his converts, a special and unique relationship. He served them without charge or salary (1 Cor. 9:6) and the right to financial support (1 Cor. 9:12). He was genuinely interested in them more than in personal gain or comfort: "For I wrote you out of great distress and anguish of heart and with many tears, not to grieve you but to let you know the depth of my love for you" (2 Cor. 2:4).

We must build credibility before we confront. Even though we may have the best credentials and reputation, we need to convince the skeptical we are trustworthy. Parishioners told me of a pastor who "wasn't honest," by which they meant that he had a hidden agenda. We establish credibility through open conversation, visiting, being vulnerable, communicating our goals clearly, and showing a genuine interest in people. We establish trust when we walk with the congregation through hardships, trials, and sorrow. That is why confrontational preaching should not take place during the first week, the first month, or perhaps even the first year of a pastorate. If trauma occurs while we are serving a church, the degree of past confidence and credibility will determine the effectiveness of confrontational preaching.

In my denomination there are no interim pastors, but retired ministers are called to serve troubled churches. These men have denominational credibility, experience, and wisdom. A retired minister friend of mine went to a small church that regularly chewed up and spit out one preacher after another. But this friend is seventy years old, has a fine reputation throughout the denomination, and is a good preacher with organizational strengths. Through his preaching he has been able to serve this church effectively and even confront them helpfully. The basis for this measure of healing is mutual trust.

Preach Issues

"Don't evade the issues, don't be wishy-washy, don't be afraid to confront." This advice comes from one of my questionnaire respondents. Many others said they found it unwise to mention names or groups of people in confrontational preaching. There is a time and place for confronting specific individuals with respect to specific behavior. In 1 Corinthians 5:1 Paul refers to a specific situation and recommends severe treatment, since the issue has become a public problem. Yet he seldom mentions the names of people to be admonished, although he does speak to Euodia and Syntyche in Philippians 4:2. More often he mentions issues of concern: worldliness, jealousy, pride, and quarreling. These are at the heart of church conflicts. We should take up these issues, directing the congregation to biblical solutions for sinful behavior.

The Old Testament prophets repeatedly confronted Israel on very specific issues. Amos addressed the oppression of the poor (Amos 4:1), materialism (3:15), injustice (2:6), and prostitution (2:7). These issues led to conflict, degeneration, and disruption in Israel.

Jesus also addressed issues. Among others, he preached on hypocrisy (Matt. 6:5), an unforgiving attitude (5:23–26), blaming others for trouble (7:3–5), unfair judgments (7:1–2), and the "I won't change" syndrome (7:24–27).

Suppose the issue in your church is partisanship. A group of people is working to "liberalize" the church. They want to allow women preachers in the pulpit and homosexuals on the church board, and they take a moderate view of the inerrancy of Scripture. Others are pulling in the opposite direction. Name-calling has begun: words like "liberal" and "Bible doubter" or "fundamentalist" and "traditionalist" are hurled back and forth. This controversy, already raging in your denomination, has now reached your church, but you want healing and harmony. Will you mention the names of the denominational leaders in this conflict and those in your church? Or will you tackle the issues through Spirit-powered preaching to set forth in clear terms the biblical teachings on these issues?

Tackle the issues, not the persons.

Preach Solutions

Joel King's church was increasingly riddled with conflict. He himself didn't help the situation: he turned every sermon into a scolding session. Sunday after Sunday he berated his people from the pulpit. Some wondered how to get rid of Pastor Joel, others schemed to accomplish it. Joel had his loyal fans who applied his tirades to those they thought needed it. Conflict began to build as he continued his "black stocking" preaching. The atmosphere was tense and depressing; worship was joyless; celebration vanished—because Pastor Joel never went beyond scolding.

Confrontation can be valuable. But we must reach beyond confrontation and preach hope. If we want our churches to go beyond the problem, we need to give the people answers. Our preaching should convince the people that it is really God who is confronting them. Careful exposition of the Bible, pointing to God as the offended party, makes people realize his stake in the matter.

Let's look at God's confrontational style. When God confronts, he never abandons his children, leaving them in the pit of despair. He always holds out to them his grace and love. Even to sinful Israel he promised restoration, forgiveness, and blessing (Isa. 40:1–2). We must preach about more than issues when we confront our churches. We must tell them repeatedly that there is forgiveness, a way out, a path for healing and restoration.

Confronting is not condemning. Condemning is pointing people to their faults without offering hope. Jesus did not condemn the woman caught in adultery. To do so would have meant his approval of the self-righteous attitude of the Pharisees. Instead, Jesus confronted the woman with her sin, offering hope through forgiveness. Confronting is facing up to the issues and declaring what Christ can do to resolve it.

When Paul pointed out the sins of the Corinthian church, he also told them of "the most excellent way" (1 Cor. 12:31). That sort of confrontation message led to godly sorrow and repentance (2 Cor. 7:8–10). Such a positive response brought recovery with no regrets for the sorrow. Confrontation gets results like that when issues are clothed in the garments of grace. The ultimate solution to conflict is the healing, restoring grace of God.

Perhaps we have preached but no change has occurred. That may happen. I have found that some people do not change even when confronted about immoral behavior. This intransigence is not because God's Spirit or his Word are impotent or inadequate; it is caused by stubbornness and pride. Often Israel refused to return to the Lord because they were a "stubborn and rebellious" people. Yet we must not despair: God's grace can change the most stubborn heart.

This is precisely where Christ can do a marvelous work in our own lives. We need Jesus no less than these stubborn people in our congregations. We have no right to scorn those who are scornful. We must model the patient, long-suffering love of our merciful God and ask God to give us the kind of love that surpasses all understanding.

Preach Cautiously

Are there dangers to confrontational preaching? Indeed there are. We should be aware of them.

The first pitfall is repeated confrontation. Suppose for some time now we have confronted the church with the issues involved in the conflict. Nothing has happened. Bitterness remains. People hold their ground, unwilling to change. So we decide to hammer away until we get the concept through their thick skulls.

That decision may do great damage. We will fail to give our church a balanced biblical diet. Remember that church life is more than struggling with conflict. It is celebrating baptisms, weddings, anniversaries, successful surgeries, and graduations. Opening the conflict wound too often will prohibit it from healing. A child who is repeatedly chastised for his behavior stops listening; admonition loses its force. Congregations learn to ignore warnings.

Another danger we face is expressing our own anger and frustration. It is easy to castigate the congregation, be aloof to the hurts of the people, and ignore their problems. Is there a tinge of anger in the soul that comes sneaking out in our sermons? Do we try to vindicate ourselves?

This raises the issue of the legitimacy of anger in the pulpit. In his book *Preaching Through a Storm,* H. Beecher Hicks, Jr., offers several sermons he preached while his church was in conflict. In an epilogue to one of them he writes, "If the reader detects in this sermon a hint of anger, the perception is accurate. I am of the opinion that one need not be ashamed of or apologetic for righteous indignation at obvious assaults upon one's integrity and motives. The congregation has a right to know that the preacher has a responsibility to communicate that such assaults will not be blithely accommodated."[3]

Now, of course there is appropriate and inappropriate anger. This normal emotion needs to be expressed—but always in biblically acceptable ways. One Christian counselor suggests that there are three essential forms of anger: rage, resentment, and righteous indignation. Of these, only the last may be biblically acceptable.[4] Personal vindictiveness, a wrathful, irascible spirit, and a desire for revenge are all expressions of the first or the second form, and all are thus unacceptable. When issues such as justice, integrity, honesty, truthfulness, and obedience are being considered, it may be appropriate to speak with righteous indignation. We must discern whether we are angry because of our pride or because of the honor of God.

Can we be angry and not know it? I know a pastor who served a church with enthusiasm and vision. When he received an opportunity to serve elsewhere, he left abruptly and swiftly, leaving no doubt he was thoroughly disgusted. The church had not responded to his leadership as he wished, and his dreams were unfulfilled. He was angry during that pastorate, but never admitted it. His smiles covered latent anger. His inability to admit to his anger prevented Christ's healing love to be shown to the pastor as well as to the church.

Paul was obviously agitated when he wrote,

> Already you have all you want! Already you have become rich! You have become kings—and that without us! How I wish that you really had become kings so that we might be kings with you! (1 Cor. 4:8).

Is our anger justifiable or is it due to a personal pique? Are we self-righteous in our indignation? We must understand the source of our emotions.

We can easily polarize the congregation through confrontation, resulting in a "they versus us" division in the church. Everyone who is involved in the trauma should be addressed in the confrontation. Taking sides, singling out individuals, and placing blame on certain people are dangers to avoid.

It is possible to denigrate a church, to beat it into the ground and remove all hope of recovery. A minister once told me the church he served was the worst in all his ministry. If he conveys this opinion in subtle ways to his congregation as he confronts them—and he probably will—they will be deeply hurt. Often people in such churches are discouraged, full of guilt, and joyless. They want to know whether there is any use continuing. In confronting them, don't leave them without hope. With God there are always new beginnings. Confrontation without hope is a serious mistake.

Preach Creatively

Are we ready to confront our congregation? How we do so will be crucial.

We might take the direct approach. Paul did this when he wrote to the Corinthians. The advantage to doing so is that everyone knows what the problem is and what the solution is. Issues are clear, the remedy transparent. The approach offers openness and frankness about the conflict. But if we take Paul's approach, we need to remember what I said earlier about trust. Paul confronted out of love in a brotherly spirit. He told the Corinthians how thankful he was for them, called them "sanctified in Christ Jesus," and repeatedly addressed them as "brothers."

This kind of confrontation demands a high degree of understanding, a deep love communicated over some time to the people, and words well chosen to convey one's thoughts. It should be with some pain that we confront, not glee and delight. Remember God's language regarding Israel? "How can I give you up, Ephraim? How can I hand you over, Israel? . . . My heart is changed within me; all my compassion is aroused" (Hos. 11:8). If done in the right spirit, people will usually respond, and if they do, we have taken a big step toward healing the church.

We can also take the indirect approach. Jesus used this method when he told stories and parables. It might prove helpful to make a study of all the confrontations of the Lord. Some were direct, some not.

Take the parable of the tenants, for example. A man planted a vineyard, rented it, and went away. At harvest time he sent servants to collect the fruit, but they were beaten and sent home. Finally he sent his son, thinking they would respect him. Instead they murdered him so they could take possession of the vineyard when the owner died. What will the owner of the vineyard do when he returns? He will come and kill the tenants and give the vineyard to others.

Those who heard Jesus tell the story felt its barb. They were stung and said, "May this never be!" The episode ended with the teachers of the law and the chief priests looking for a way to arrest Jesus because "they knew he had spoken this parable against them" (Luke 20:9–19).

Jesus made his point effectively by indirect confrontation. The Scriptures contain many examples of this type of encounter: Nathan confronting David (2 Sam. 12); Jesus confronting the Samaritan woman (John 4); Paul confronting the Greeks on Mars Hill (Acts 17). We too can use stories, figures, illustrations, and other literary devices to make a point.

A Confrontational Sermon

I preached the following sermon, an example of confrontational preaching, after I had served a wounded church for ten years. To understand the impact, allow me to set it in context.

I came to the church after two pastors had left. One had led a group of people out of the church, the result of a conflict in "philosophy of ministry." The other also left with some hard feelings. There were deep hurts and a depressed spirit in the congregation. During the next ten years things had come together quite well in the church. The membership had changed, the leadership was enthusiastic, and a good spirit prevailed. In preparation for this book I decided to ask the people through a questionnaire what part preaching played in this recovery.

Although the results were positive, a minority of six percent reacted negatively, some with unsubstantiated accusations. Meanwhile, the director of education and youth, unordained but licensed to preach, conducted a service while I was on vacation. A few people walked out of this service in displeasure for no good reason. These incidents made me reflect on the problem of insubordination in the congregation. The purpose of the sermon I preached was to set forth the biblical truth about who may preach and what the benefits of preaching are. The goal was to change this unbiblical behavior in the church.

✳   ✳   ✳

Sermon: "Your Response to Preaching"

Scripture Reading: Romans 10:1–21
Text: Romans 10:14–15

> How, then, can they call on the one they have not believed
> in? And how can they believe in the one of whom they have
> not heard? And how can they hear without someone
> preaching to them? And how can they preach unless they are
> sent?

Dear Fellow Believers

As the bulletin today indicates, Ida and I have been with you
for exactly ten years. Since our coming, I have preached approxi-
mately eight hundred sermons from this pulpit. Last week I sat back
and asked myself, "What have all these sermons accomplished?" I
recently asked that of you in a questionnaire to see whether my
preaching had anything to do with the healing of this church. I
received two kinds of replies. Some of you said it had a great deal
to do with the healing of this church, and others said preaching had
nothing to do with it. At first this took me by surprise, but after
further reflection I understood.

Preaching is intended to affect and change people's lives. But
that doesn't always . happen. Jesus' preaching didn't change
everyone who heard him, and neither did Paul's. Peter's didn't
either, and neither does Billy Graham's. So I am not surprised that
my preaching has not always had a positive effect.

Paul speaks in Romans 9–11 of the response of the Jewish
nation to preaching: "The Word is near you; it is in your mouth
and in your heart, that is, the Word of faith we are proclaiming"
(Rom. 10:8). The Word was preached to them—but what happened? They didn't believe! Paul preached to them about Christ,
saying, "If you confess with your mouth, 'Jesus is Lord,' and
believe in your heart that God raised him from the dead, you will
be saved" (Rom. 10:9). Then he asked *how* can they call on the
one they have not believed in, *how* can they believe in the one of
whom they have not heard, then *how* can they hear without
someone preaching to them, and finally *how* can they preach
unless they are sent? I will consider these phrases in reverse order,

beginning at verse 15, "How can they preach unless they are sent?"

I. The Person Who Preaches

You will look hard and long in the New Testament for a word that describes the kind of preaching I have been doing these ten years. That is because the New Testament is a missionary book. Paul wrote several pastoral epistles to Timothy and Titus, but even these were to men serving in an evangelistic setting. When the Bible refers to preaching in the New Testament, it is almost always missionary and evangelistic preaching. The preacher is a herald. A herald in the Greek city-states was someone who announced news in the streets and summoned people to public meetings. In a world of no television, radio, or newspapers, the herald spread the news in the streets.

A preacher is someone who brings good news; he is a herald. Billy Graham brings good news, missionaries bring good news, and wherever the gospel is announced there is New Testament preaching.

The preaching I do every Sunday is not like that. What I do is closer to teaching. It is preaching directed to Christian, believing people like you. It deals with edification and instruction—informing and inspiring you. Of course, the Good News must be a part of this instruction. The grace of God in Christ is communicated through preaching. My preaching is aimed more at building up the body and equipping the saints.

In either case—whether the emphasis falls on heralding the Good News or on teaching the saints—preaching is communicating God's Word. Preaching is *proclaiming* God's Word to mankind. It is, in fact, *"official proclamation!"* How can they preach unless *they are sent?* Paul thinks of himself as an ambassador of Jesus Christ. An ambassador is someone officially sent by one country to another. A preacher is someone whom God has appointed and officially sent to convey his message to people. Ambassadors do not formulate messages of their own, but convey messages given them by higher authorities.

I became an official representative of Jesus Christ when I was ordained some thirty-two years ago. The church officially declared through its office-bearers, "Jerry, you have the gifts, knowledge, training, and the Holy Spirit. We designate you as an official proclaimer of the gospel." So I have been sent officially to preach in the church. I have those credentials.

My associate also has those credentials. Although he is not ordained, he went to the official bodies of the church, the consistory and the classis, and has obtained a license to preach. There are two of us, therefore, whom the church has approved to be Christ's official ambassadors to you. Men cannot preach "unless they are sent." The two of us have been sent to you. We have a great responsibility to bring you Christ's message and not our own. We take that very seriously.

But some of you have walked out of church or stayed at home when one of us preaches! Do you know that you are walking away from God's ambassador, someone God is sending to you with a message—a message of grace and truth? Have you thought of how offensive this might be to God? It's not that either one of us in himself is worthy of being heard, but God has chosen to speak to you through us. How can they preach unless they are sent?

II. The Person Who Hears

"How can they *hear* without a preacher?" You know who the preachers are in this church, who sends them, and how they are sent—but are you *listening* to them?

I sat in the pew these last four weeks on my vacation. I admit it was difficult to be a good listener. For me it is easier to be in the pulpit preaching than to be in the pew listening. Listening is hard work. Many of us are poor listeners. Even in our casual conversation with each other, our minds tend to wander. Whenever we observe a bored expression or a suppressed yawn, we know listening is hard. It takes concentration to observe facial expression, voice inflection, and all the clues of nonverbal communication.

In Matthew 7 Jesus places listening and obedience side by side in the story of the two builders, one of whom built on the sand and the other on the rock.

> Therefore, everyone who *hears* these words of mine and *puts them into practice* is like a wise man. . . . But everyone who *hears* these words of mine and does not *put them into practice* is like a foolish man who built his house upon the sand (Matt. 7:24, 26).

Hearing and obeying go together. You haven't heard the Word of God until you have obeyed it. "How shall they *hear* without someone preaching to them?" Someone is preaching to you every Sunday, but are you listening? You have heard a lot of words— eight hundred sermons' worth! Some of you seem to say that all this preaching had no effect upon you and the church. If that's so— you haven't been listening!

May I suggest that you mentally insert a word into your Bible? *How can they hear* . . . what word would you insert after hear— hear whom? How can they hear Jerry Gunnink? Pastor . . . ? The Reverend . . . ? Dr . . . ? Mr . . . ? Hear whom? Whoever is in the pulpit? No, that is not what Paul means. You need to hear someone much greater than any one of us. Hear God! How can you hear God without a preacher? Have you been coming to this church for ten years to hear the wrong person? No wonder you said in the questionnaire that preaching did absolutely nothing for you! You didn't come to hear God! You didn't listen for him to speak to you. You didn't tune your ears and ask, "Lord, what do you want me to hear from you today?" Evidently some of you never hear God, and the result is barren, fruitless lives. Nothing happens in your spiritual life because you haven't listened properly.

On vacation I listened to a layman preach. His text was 1 Timothy 1:1–2. As he began to preach, I began to analyze everything: his exegesis, delivery, application, and style. Then it dawned on me: I wasn't listening for God to speak to me. I was listening for correct doctrine and teaching. I felt ashamed of myself, and I began to listen with a different ear.

It doesn't matter whether I or someone else is in the pulpit. You should come to hear God. If you don't hear him, you will go home empty, sad, critical, and disillusioned.

III. *The Person Who Believes*

First, God sends someone to you who officially represents him. No one can preach unless he is *sent by God* through his church. Then God requires you to *hear that messenger* but hearing is not enough. To hear is to respond, to take the next step and *believe.* "How can they believe in one whom they have not heard?" There must be faith, true believing faith. The Heidelberg Catechism asks the question, "You confess that by faith alone you share in Christ and all his blessings. Where does that faith come from?" The answer given is, "The Holy Spirit produces it in our hearts by the *preaching* of the Holy Gospel."

If you listen for God to speak to you, he will bring you both to faith and to growth in faith. Peter writes, "For you have been born again, not of perishable seed, but of imperishable, through the living and enduring word of God" (1 Peter 1:23). You have been born again. The seed of faith has been planted in you through the preaching of the Word. God does not dispense faith where his Word is not preached. That is why we send out missionaries. When the Word is preached, the Holy Spirit uses that Word to bring new life to hearts.

Is there someone here this morning who does not have faith? Is there someone here who must say, "I am not a Christian. I don't believe?" You must listen carefully, listen for God to speak to you, listen to his voice telling you to repent of your sins, believe in God's only Son, Jesus Christ, who came to rescue you from your sins. God wants you to hear his voice saying, "I love you and want you as my child." Are you listening and believing?

If you have responded to God's call, then preaching has already had an effect on your life. The Holy Spirit not only brings you to faith, but also builds you up in your faith through preaching. Does this *always* happen? Does preaching always produce faith and build up? No! Paul asks that question regarding the Jews of his day. "Did they not hear? Of course they did!" But did they accept the preaching of Jesus Christ as Messiah? No. How often the prophets preached, but the people did not believe. "Who has believed our report?" cries Isaiah.

If you don't believe the preacher today, your life will be empty, dry, and full of hurts. You will become hardened in your heart. What you need is to be humbled, to become meek and receive what God says to you. It doesn't matter who the ambassador is, he has a message from God. *Believe* the message!

IV. The Person Who Makes a Commitment

Preaching comes full circle and achieves its purpose when a person responds and makes a commitment to God. Simply to believe and accept the message is insufficient. You must act, respond—you must do something. You must "call upon the Lord," the one in whom you believe.

Let me address those of you who are ten to twelve years of age, you who are teenagers. Have you heard about Jesus' love for you? Have you heard about his death on the cross and the life he gives? Do you believe this? More important than believing is that you call on the name of the Lord. How can you call on the Lord if you don't believe? How can you believe if you don't hear the message? How can you hear unless someone tells you? We are here to tell you. We are telling you about the love God has for you.

But are you calling on the name of God? Will you respond? Paul warns the people in Rome that the Israelites did not make a commitment to Christ as the true Messiah and, therefore, were lost. That could happen to you too. "All day long I have held out my hands to a disobedient and obstinate people" (Rom. 10:21).

Some of you have made a commitment. You have come to call on the Lord. Every sermon is a challenge for you to call on him. All eight hundred sermons I have preached from this pulpit have demanded a response from you—to grow in faith. That response may have been to be a better steward, to be faithful in prayer, to change an attitude, or to a stronger faith. Every one of my sermons had an application to your life. Each week I have placed in the bulletin suggested "application points." If you diligently study these application points, I assure you every sermon will make a difference in your life. If there are no changes, you have not been listening and believing. You are not calling on the Lord.

In the questionnaire I recently distributed, I mentioned an interim pastor who preached here shortly after the splintering of our congregation and how his preaching affected our church. Someone chided me for placing myself in the same league with him, as though I were doing that. I have never made that comparison, and I wouldn't attempt to stand in his shoes. He is a great man of God. I feel like the apostle Paul, who said,

> When I came to you, brothers, I did not come with eloquence or superior wisdom as I proclaimed to you the testimony about God. For I resolved to know nothing while I was with you except Jesus Christ and him crucified. I came to you in weakness and fear, and with much trembling. My message and my preaching were not with wise and persuasive words, but with a demonstration of the Spirit's power, so that your faith might not rest on men's wisdom, but on God's power (1 Cor. 2:1–5).

What I hear some of you say is, "I am of Mr. _____ "; others, "I am of the Reverend _____ "; and, "I am of Gunnink." Don't you see yourself in the Scriptures? Don't you see Corinth repeated in our church? Have you ever applied those verses to yourself as you pride yourself in certain men? What, after all, is Apollos? And what is Paul? And what is Gunnink? Only servants through whom you came to believe. This is why I am here. That is why I have preached eight hundred sermons from this pulpit.

What has this preaching done for you? Nothing? I have literally wept tears about that. But I also warn you that it is very dangerous to come here Sunday after Sunday and not hear God and respond by believing, calling on God in repentance. You may have thought you were listening to Gunnink all these years, but if you didn't hear God, you missed all eight hundred sermons!

✳   ✳   ✳

This sermon was well received. Those who responded to me personally said, "That was for me! I needed that!" Those who absented themselves when my associate preached were now present, and those who walked out did so no more. The church became calm. Everyone knew an important issue had been dealt with and a solution given. Some elders remarked that this sermon was a turning point in the life of the church. Further recovery will depend on the grace of God.

6

Pastoral Preaching

Your church is hemorrhaging. How can you save it from dying from the deep gashes of conflict? Obviously you need to exercise pastoral care over your congregation. But the pastoral work alone will not heal the church. You must also preach pastorally. Healing can occur only when preaching and pastoral care are combined.

What is pastoral preaching? According to Charles F. Kemp, it is "an attempt to meet the individual and personal needs of the people by means of a sermon. It is an attempt to take the needs of the people in one hand and the truth of the gospel in the other and bring the two together by means of the spoken word."[1] Robert D. Dale said, "Pastoral preaching always brings theology and the Bible into focus on the felt needs of the people in the pews."[2] The preacher has one eye on God's people, "the sheep of his pasture," and the other on the Bible, the pastureland in which they feed. The chief concern in pastoral preaching is to apply salve where it hurts most.

Although all preaching intends to address the needs of the congregation, a wounded church has special concerns. Its needs are intensified and multiplied. This makes preaching in such a church much more challenging.

Determining the Needs of a Church

A colleague recently came to a church in serious conflict. He decided that the church needed a new vision, an outreach program, something to make the church grow. He thought he should divert attention from the trauma, forgetting the past and pressing on into new ministry. He taught, preached, and worked to implement this concept as the way to heal his church.

Although it seemed to him a logical strategy to change the focus, it did not work. When he realized how sick the church was, he changed his approach. Like a patient in a hospital who needs rest and recovery, this church needed time to heal. It was in no condition to reach out to others. Church members needed first to be reconciled, forgiven, and restored. Denying problems does not heal churches. This minister wisely changed his approach when he discovered the needs of the congregation and began to address them. What are the pressing demands of your church? How can you determine what they are?

Listening

I asked hundreds of pastors serving traumatized churches what they found most helpful in determining the needs of their churches. Almost universally they identified "listening." Listen to former pastors, interim pastors, colleagues, and above all to the people. Listen to leaders on both sides of the issue, especially those involved in the trouble. Listen at committee meetings, board meetings, after church, and in conversations on the golf course, at the bowling alley, or over a cup of coffee. Always be listening for clues about what bothers people. Visit people in their homes. Some pastors literally visit every home to listen to the parishioners' stories. We cannot remain in our studies and preach pastorally. Pastoral sermons derive their context from people's lives.

Listen for the tone of voice, facial expression, body action, gestures, and signs of tension. I listened to one person who, sitting on the edge of the chair, shaking his clenched fist with vigor, shouting, shifting, staring, told me what was bothering him. As I listened I saw how deeply the problem affected him.

Others are not as obvious about their needs. They cover their hurts with smiles, but the pain is just as real. Concentration and alertness will enable us to listen for their concerns. Even when the people in the pew cannot consciously articulate those needs, we can.

Let me illustrate. As I write, a pastor I know is preaching on what he considers to be the issues in our denomination. These include whether women should be ordained in church offices, biblical inerrancy, the interpretation of Genesis, and other matters. He has become highly critical of certain publications, positions, and people. Sunday after Sunday he attacks one issue after another. Divisions are developing in his church as people take sides on the issues. Some consider him to be a champion of orthodoxy while others absent themselves from the church. Here is trauma in the making.

What's wrong? Why is this happening? Shouldn't there be any preaching on issues? Of course. But we must first ask whether this is the pressing need of *your* church. Is there erosion in your church on the doctrine of biblical inerrancy? Are the people entertaining false ideas about the origin of the universe? Are these the issues disturbing your congregation, or do they only disturb you? Is your congregation divided over these issues? Then you may have to address them. But that young pastor I know has his own agenda and doesn't think about the needs of his flock. What does our flock require in distinction from every other flock? Careful assessment through listening will help us preach pastorally.

Consult the Leadership

All churches should have times of celebration, encouragement, admonition, and instruction. Strife-torn churches need discipline, love, forgiveness, and acceptance. To determine the exact needs of our congregation we should consult the responsible leadership. They ought to have some insight into the exact needs at a particular stage of the trauma. There is this caution, however, not to use them as an the only source of our information. The leadership may be biased. It may be dominated by specific individuals who wield power. We need to listen and assess leadership input.

History

Carefully examine the history of the congregation. We must ask ourselves many questions. Have there been previous conflicts in the church? How were they begun, who was involved, how was it resolved, if ever? Have previous ministers had difficulty in this church? Have ministers who served acceptably elsewhere had difficulty here? Sometimes the principle cause of trauma is the minister, at other times unresolved problems in the membership. Some churches have a history of conflict. Study and analyze the congregation through its history.

Questionnaire

I recently used a computerized questionnaire formulated by Church Data Services to uncover problems.[3] This organization found that the leadership sometimes miscalculates the condition of the church. For example, the leadership of one church estimated training in evangelism to be ninth in a list of ten needs while the congregation listed it as the first need. In my own case, introducing a family night had caused considerable friction in the church at first. But when we asked the people in the questionnaire to evaluate this program, eighty-four percent supported it; so there was no great need to address this issue further. Moreover, the survey brought to light several strengths in the church, such as a caring fellowship, meaningful worship, good preaching, and faithful stewardship. The needs also became evident as people expressed through the questionnaire a desire for greater intimacy, training in prayer, and more effective use of spiritual gifts. This survey enabled me to address the specific needs of the church.

A well-conceived survey can reveal much about individual needs, family needs, church effectiveness, and the value of our preaching. Whatever method we use, we must be sure it will disclose accurate perceptions and uncover the true needs of the church.

Determining Individual Needs

Pastoral preaching is not a smorgasbord intended to satisfy everyone's palate all the time. It is a special-order diet for people with unique needs. Some people may not be able to relate to the conflict. For example, a husband and wife may be going through a difficult divorce. Their needs will be entirely different from those involved in the church conflict. But in their case, this personal problem will be factored into the conflict as they participate in its resolution. Remember, our preaching must cover all aspects of congregational life. There will be births, deaths, marriages, children, young people, sick people, unemployed, lonely, and angry people. Preach to all the needs of all the people.

At the same time, some people will be weathering the raging storm in specific ways. They will be asking questions such as, Shall I go to church this morning? Shall I go to a neighboring church? How can I pray? Forgive? Be reconciled? Shall I leave my denomination? Speak my convictions? May I break bread with my opponents at the next commemoration of the Lord's Supper? These are disturbing questions that beg for a word from God to guide and instruct.

Young people and children face unique difficulties in a strife-torn church. Many have told me of their hurts and questions: "Why do people fight about building a new church or where to locate it? Why don't people love each other if they love the Lord? Why do they have disputes over various teachings that are not explicitly taught in Scripture? I hate all this bickering." Idealistic young people have a hard time with tensions, alienation, and arguing about things they think unimportant. We must preach biblically and sensitively in ways that consider the young people's confusion over the trauma.

One pastor observed a small group of obstructionistic and reactionary people in his church. They displayed antisocial behavior and more than a little opposition to the leadership. By listening, reading history, and observing these people, he concluded they were angry because they had lost control and power in the church. They felt alienated when their ideas were not implemented. They had been a source of trouble for many years. He preached sermons on anger (Eph. 4:26, 31), grief (a sense of loss), servanthood (Matt. 23:11– 12), humility (Phil. 2:1–8), foot washing (John 13:14–15), and several topics from 1 Corinthians. These sermons helped to change the behavior of the affected people. The pastor was influential because he was a loving shepherd who listened, understood human nature, and applied the Bible to their situation. This is pastoral preaching that heals.

Distinguishing Needs

As pastors we need to learn to distinguish between denial of needs, felt needs, and unfelt needs. These distinctions are helpful in diagnosing the church.

After ten years in a conflict-laden congregation, one person said, "We never had a problem here." Some never become involved in the trouble; they deny it is even happening. It is tempting to suppress conflict and to think all is well. Some pastors also deny any conflict in their church or fail to consider that they may be the cause of it. Denial, however, does not eliminate problems.

Apparently the congregation at Corinth denied some of their problems. In a statement of irony Paul writes, "Already you have all you want! Already you have become rich! You have become kings—and that without us" (1 Cor. 4:8)! They acted as if everything were under control. Paul knew differently.

Felt needs demand immediate attention. They are urgent, conscious, surface needs. People will verbalize these to us.

Unfelt needs are the unspoken, unarticulated, and usually more fundamental needs. Discerning these will be more difficult. But doing so will enable us to preach pastorally.

The Felt And Unfelt Needs of the Church

A church, like the individuals in it, usually looks for easy ways out of a dilemma. The people hope a new pastor will quickly solve the problems with his winsome personality, good preaching, and new ideas. "Pastor," someone once said to me, "your work is cut out for you. See these empty pews?" It was obvious that the church wanted to attract new members, grow, and thereby demonstrate that it was healthy. But was that the real need?

The Corinthian congregation wrote to Paul expressing felt needs (1 Cor. 7:1). They wanted to solve the problem of a marriage in which one member was converted to the Christian faith but the other was not. Another felt need was to know whether people should eat meat sacrificed to idols (1 Cor. 8:1). These were surface desires demanding an immediate answer. While not neglecting these, Paul reached deeper and dealt with their lack of love.

We will quickly discover felt needs when we enter a traumatized church. They clamor for attention and resolution. We should preach to these shouting demands. Paul did. In fact, we may not be able to get at the real underlying needs until we have dealt sufficiently with these surface needs. We must feed a hungry man before we can quench his thirsty soul.

I found that the immediate need in my church was encouragement. The church had lost its fervor, enthusiasm, and joy. As several attempts to obtain a minister failed, a feeling of despair grew. My first task was to instill hope into this church. When the people expressed surprise that I would even come, I reminded them of God's faithfulness and love. I told them I would preach a great deal about the love of God. Taking my cue from Paul, who always gave encouragement and commendation when he addressed the churches, I did the same. This preaching helped to form a base from which to launch into the unfelt needs.

Learn to go beyond the obvious. Paul received insight into the situation in the Corinthian church from Chloe, Stephanus, Fortunatus, and Achaicus. He found that the deeper needs were, divisions and quarrels (1:10–11), worldliness and Christian immaturity (3:1–3), discipline (5:11), lawsuits among believers (6:1–6), sexual immorality (6:9–20), improper celebration of the Lord's Supper (10:14ff.; 11:17ff.), spiritual gifts (chaps. 12–14), and doctrinal deviation regarding the resurrection of the body (chap. 15). To what extent the people realized these as their basic problems is uncertain. Paul addressed them to promote health in the body.

What are the underlying problems in our church? Is it a proper view of the church, acceptance of divergent viewpoints, forgiveness, discipline, harmony, tolerance, false doctrine, humility? To help our people discern such needs, we might preach a series of sermons on Revelation 2 and 3. Each of the seven churches described there has weaknesses and strengths to which people can relate today. Pastoral preaching does not ignore either the strengths of a congregation or its weaknesses.

The Felt and Unfelt Needs of Individuals

Arthur Teikmanis writes, "Psychological studies have revealed that it is hard for us to conquer malice, vengeance, and hate because behind them are repressed resentments, frustrations, and pride. People who feel that life has denied them their due are bound to remain prisoners of vengeance and hate."[4] We will have little difficulty detecting the surface issues bothering people; they will tell them to us. But it will take some digging and analyzing to discover the underlying causes of a person's behavior.

Some have great difficulty submitting to authority. Others press for their viewpoint as the only option as they seek to mask fear and insecurity. Some are constantly embroiled in controversy. Others are overly aggressive, intolerant, and belligerent. Then again, there are those who are too tolerant, passive, and immature to resolve conflict. We as their pastors are the diagnosticians. From the background, history, and knowledge of each person, we determine the felt and unfelt needs. We must ask ourselves questions such as, What has shaped this person's life? Has he been abused, ignored, rejected? Why does he act this way? How has he learned to respond to difficulties? Are there factors of which he is not even aware?

When parishioners blister us in anger, dump on us the responsibility for the problems of the church, challenge our integrity and ability to minister effectively, we need to stop and ask some of these questions about them. I know a minister who becomes defensive, fights back, and argues with a person like that. This response results in a full-scale war. How much more godly to attend to the other person's deep needs. Has this person been ignored in the past? Does he lack love and attention? Is he covering up a spiritual problem? Our challenge is to act to change this person's destructive behavior to constructive behavior. To do so, we must preach lovingly about the rewards of humble service and the joys of working for Christ. We need to exhibit that behavior ourselves. Our preaching will be most effective when we have a personal, pastoral relationship with such people. We must show these individuals that we love them.

Catching the Vision

Consider the following scene. A shepherd is caring for his sheep in a quiet, grassy meadow. His dog lies beside him; the sheep are content, satisfied, and unafraid. A clean, rippling brook meanders gently through the valley. The shepherd is relaxed on the hillside. Is this a picture of your flock and you as shepherd?

Wouldn't it be wonderful if all congregations could be portrayed so idyllically? But we know that isn't the picture of most congregations, and surely not of a strife-torn church!

The scene is more like a lion, bear, or wild animal attacking the sheep. The flock is scattering, the sheep are fearful, some are wounded. The wolf of conflict is making huge gashes in sheep, and they are bleeding.

Up on your feet, shepherd! Care for those sheep (John 10:12–13). God holds you accountable for them (Ezek. 34). If necessary, with great personal sacrifice lay down your life for the sheep. Make their hurts yours. Their tears, yours. There will be agony, pain, and suffering in your preaching. Imitate your Shepherd-God who "tends his flock like a shepherd: he gathers the lambs in his arms and carries them close to his heart; he gently leads those that have young" (Isa. 40:11). Learn from Moses, whose flock was traumatized most of the time (Ex. 32:31–32). Think of Jesus the Great Shepherd of the sheep (Heb. 13:20), who agonized, "O, Jerusalem, Jerusalem, you who kill the prophets and stone those sent to you, how often I have longed to gather your children together, as a hen gathers her chicks under her wings, but you were not willing" (Matt. 23:37). Paul even wished himself cursed and cut off from Christ for the sake of his brothers (Rom. 9:3).

Pastoral preaching flows only from the mouth of a preacher who enters into the painful life of his people. We cannot stand aloof and mechanically dispense spiritual pain pills. Our preaching must show the signs of struggle; that we have experienced the sorrows, wounds, and burdens of our people. Whatever it takes—soft love, tough love, rejected love—our commitment to our flock is primary. Preach them through their trauma by believing that "God will meet all your needs according to his glorious riches in Christ Jesus" (Phil. 4:19).

In the next chapter I will prescribe a special diet for feeding a wounded flock. Only carefully planned preaching can heal a flock. We shall have to consider how to develop such preaching.

Comprehensive Preaching

In surveying sixty-three pastors I asked them to list two or three biblical passages and themes they found most helpful in preaching for recovery. Not surprisingly, the list included a wide range of texts. No single passage or group of passages is sufficient. From my own experience I had concluded that a full range of biblical preaching is needed. There are a number of reasons why we should preach from a broad range of biblical truth.

Reasons for Preaching Comprehensively

The Issues Involved

The diagram of a church fight is seldom narrow or specific. Implications and ramifications are varied. People experience the conflict many ways: substantively, intrapersonally, and interpersonally.[1] For instance, let's suppose the quarrel is about the interpretation of Genesis 1. This is a substantive issue and involves facts, interpretation of Scripture, and science. The issue arises, however, in the context of someone who challenges the traditional or commonly accepted view. From here it moves to the interprersonal area. Personal attacks are made on the one who advances new theories. People choose sides and rally behind leaders.

If one were to delve further into the nature of the

conflict, it would become evident that certain people are always on either the conservative or the progressive side of any issue. The conflict now has an intrapersonal dimension. An inner alarm is triggered when something new appears. Others are impatient, always formulating some new concept. People often live according to cherished assumptions of which they are unaware. This is important to know for preaching. We may address the *issue* of the interpretation of Genesis and think we have solved the problem. But that is too simplistic. We must also deal with personal and interpersonal matters.

How can a person accept—and even love—another with whom he has sharp differences when inner feelings are aroused at the very mention of his name? Pride may enter the picture, a person's conscience may pull him to the conservative side, or a desire to be accepted by a certain group may lead him toward the progressives. He may have ambivalence, and inner struggle. How do we preach to problems like that? By preaching the whole counsel of God.

Consider the other related issues. Is it important to "make every effort to keep the unity of the Spirit through the bond of peace" (Eph. 4:3)? Should we preach on "always learning but never able to acknowledge the truth" (2 Tim. 3:7)? Will we preach on submission to authorities, rightly dividing the Word of truth, counting others better than ourselves, patience, the faithfulness of God, encouragement, judging, fighting the good fight, and a host of other subjects? We would be wise to do so. This list could be expanded. Do not merely address the issue; also address the persons who have become identified with the issue. The conflict in a church has many aspects to it; that is why we must tackle the trauma from many sides. Do not make the mistake of harping on one thing, hoping that will solve the problem.

The Time Factor

Another reason for preaching the full range of Christian truth is the time factor. Recovery from strife takes time.

Wounds don't heal overnight. Depending on the causes of trauma and all the variables that go into a church conflict, recovery may take as long as several years.

If a minister who caused the conflict resigns or moves to another church, the recovery period may be very short. If, however, the church is woefully divided and people have chosen sides, recovery probably will take much longer. Forgiveness doesn't come easily or quickly. As Lewis Smedes points out, "It takes time; a lot of time for some. Sometimes you struggle with it so long that you cannot remember the moment you finally did it."[2]

I remember a meeting of the church membership at which a budget matter was being discussed. It involved a ministry in which the church had been engaged for many years, but which had become controversial. When one member spoke of the history of this ministry with sadness, another person new to the church said, "That's all past and we should forget it." The former person replied, "You weren't here when this happened, but many of us were, and it still hurts."

People do not easily forget. And if they do not forgive, it is virtually impossible to forget a serious trauma. The wound is often lanced only to bleed again. Meanwhile, we must preach each Sunday to a congregation working through their pain and grief.

Since time is important to the healing process, preach about many different subjects while allowing recovery to take place gradually. The pastors serving strife-torn churches indicated in my survey that they avoided "quick-fix" approaches, "easy answers," "moving too quickly," and "trying to hurry the healing process." Unless we serve the same dish each Sunday, it will be essential to deal with a variety of themes over a span of time. This also means that we ought to remain in a church for as much time as it takes to bring healing and recovery.

Developing a New Vision

Comprehensive preaching allows for the development of a new vision for ministry. It is a mistake to focus exclusively and exhaustively on causes of the church's trauma. To make recovery happen, the church must gain a new vision of how it can become a center for ministry. Its attention must be drawn to broader aspects of Christian living—the kingdom of God, spiritual warfare, discipleship, the holiness of God.

Often the congregation needs a new vision of God himself. This can be accomplished through preaching. Preach about worship, evangelism, fellowship, social action, contemporary problems: all the regular growth issues. Preaching these themes broadens the church's vision. Help them to see the bigger picture, the broader horizons. Provide a panoramic view of the faith. People tend to become myopic in conflict and see only immediate problems; they think everything hinges on a quick resolution of the conflict.

Since it is painful to live with conflict, many will want to dismiss it as soon as possible. The Band-Aid approach seldom succeeds. Preaching on a few verses or passages may temporarily anesthetize against pain, but it is sure to return. Healing takes time. Preaching comprehensively and inclusively dilutes the conflict by placing it within the context of the whole range of Christian living.

Balancing Our Perception

Covering the major themes of Scripture balances our perception of the conflict. We all tend to exaggerate problems. When discord exists, everything gets interpreted in terms of the conflict. Some years ago a young person in my church began to grow long hair and a beard, which at the time were identified with unconventional behavior and rock music groups. Since he was an usher, some people were offended and refused to be ushered in by him. Pressure was applied to the elders of the church to remove him from his position, and he was asked to resign. Fortunately, the man did not react negatively or become belligerent, but accepted the decision of the elders. Today he is a professor in a Christian college.

For some people, not growing a beard or having long hair is a standard by which to judge authentic faith and test orthodoxy. The same thing may happen when people replace the King James Version's "thee" and "thou" address to God with "you." Such matters can easily breed conflict. People exaggerate and lose a balanced view of a wholesome Christian life. Preaching in those situations must draw people away from preconceived perceptions to authentic Christianity. Preaching comprehensively brings greater balance to people's lives.

As pastors we too may develop a distorted and exaggerated perception of the conflict. We may build one small, insignificant factor into an insurmountable mountain, such as criticism of a minor point in a sermon or our clothes or our spouse. From then on we will see everything through the lens of that experience. If gossip is the problem, we will be tempted to concentrate on this sin in every sermon. We need a biblical eye exam—to correct our distorted vision. Don't be caught preaching to a "certain group of people" in the congregation year after year thinking, *They need to hear this!* Although specific issues should be addressed at the appropriate time, the point here is that comprehensive preaching keeps things in balance for both the congregation and the preacher.

The Wholeness of Life

The tentacles of conflict reach down to the roots of people's lives. Seldom does conflict affect only one part of life. Church fights are not abstract intellectual exercises, but intensely emotional experiences. People think of leaving the church, breaking off long-standing relationships. Conflict affects the total person: all areas of Christian living, such as prayer life, worship of God, treatment of others, involvement in the church, perceptions of the church, personal attitudes, and a host of other matters pertaining to everyday life. People may even question God, doubt his promises, feel abandoned by him, and become depressed. This is why we should address a wide range of issues. Covering the full range of Christian doctrine encompasses the wholeness of life for every believer.

Of course it is also true that people have varying needs and react differently to trauma. Some have to deal with anger, others with fear. Besides the individual wants there are the overarching necessities everyone has. All need the grace of God, reconciliation, the tenderness of the Holy Spirit, the readiness to do battle with the forces of evil (Eph. 6), or the strength to love according to 1 Corinthians 13.

James points out the interrelatedness of life; he says all the commandments hang together for life is a whole.

> If you really keep the royal law found in Scripture, "Love your neighbor as yourself," you are doing right. But if you show favoritism, you sin and are convicted by the law as lawbreakers. For whoever keeps the whole law and yet stumbles at just one point is guilty of breaking all of it (James 2:8–10).

A good pastor will address the whole person—mind, will, and affections—with the whole counsel of God. To teach only to issue-oriented needs is insufficient. To demand action without proper training about implementation lacks effectiveness. Moreover, our members must come to know, experience, and grasp the love and compassion of God. Motivate them as well as help them understand what they must do to bring recovery to their church. Comprehensive preaching alone enables such recovery to take place.

Major Themes

What will we include in the diet for our churches? What did other pastors find most helpful?

The Church

Many pastors find that preaching on various aspects of the doctrine of the church is helpful. A proper understanding of the nature, purpose, and polity of the church enables them to place the conflict in a biblical context of what the church is. The following themes on the church were suggested in the survey responses:

"The Church Belongs To Christ"
"The Nature of the Church"
"Jesus' Healing Power Builds His Church"
"Respect for the Offices of the Church"
"Equipping Members for the Work of the Church"
"Unity and Diversity in the Church"
"The Inclusive Church"
"The Beauty and Glory of the Church of Christ"
"The Church as the Body of Christ"
"My Church is Worthy Because . . . "
"The Mission of the Church"
"Church Renewal"
"Fellowship in Christ's Church"

In our preaching we should emphasize the true owner and preserver of the church (Matt. 16:18). Proclaim Christ as head (Eph. 1:22). Use Hebrews 13:17 to show that members must obey their leaders and submit to their authority. Preach unity in the church from Ephesians 4:3: "Make every effort to keep the unity of the Spirit through the bond of peace." Picture the beauty and glory of the church from Ephesians 5:25–32 and show that she is the very bride of Christ (Rev. 21:9). Trace renewal in the Scriptures from a number of Old Testament passages like Jeremiah 6:16; 2 Chronicles 30:20–24; and Psalm 80:19. Use 1 Corinthians 12 in stressing diversity in unity. We may want to deal with 1 Corinthians 11:19: "No doubt there have to be differences among you to show which of you have God's approval."

Donald MacNair, an author and consultant, believes it is important to teach the doctrines of accountability and submission in a church fight, along with principles that govern the polity and life of the church. Indeed, Scripture is useful for teaching, rebuking, correcting, and training in righteousness (2 Tim. 3:16).

The Holy Spirit

Because it is the Holy Spirit who must heal the church, preach sermons on who he is and what he does. We might have a series of sermons on spiritual gifts (Rom. 12:3–8; 1 Cor. 12), stressing the importance of each person in the church. We can show how each person is needed, is useful, and must contribute to the common good. A healthy church is like an orchestra with many instruments playing the same piece of beautiful music.

The Spirit also produces fruit in our lives, according to Galatians 5:22–23. Without this fruit, the church will not recover. Spend time expounding and applying each fruit— love, joy, peace, patience, kindness, goodness, faithfulness, gentleness, self-control. As people exhibit these, harmony will develop.

Study the anointing of the Holy Spirit. Trace the anointings of Saul and David and the effects on their lives. Examine the Lord's anointing at his baptism, equipping him for ministry (Luke 4:14, 18), and preparing him for temptation (Luke 4:1, 14). The Holy Spirit is similarly indispensable to us as we minister to each other and resist temptations in the midst of conflict.

Proclaim the life-bringing work of the Spirit. Is the strife in our church fanned by people who are not born again? Is it predominantly a spiritual problem? Of course there will be conflict if some people are not renewed by the Spirit. Don't assume that just because they are members, they have the life of the Spirit (John 3:7; Rom. 8:6). So preach for conversion.

The Kingdom of God

The kingdom of God is one of the largest concepts in Scripture. Preaching through the Sermon on the Mount (Matt. 5–7) might seem a long exercise, but if done over a period of time it will give the people an idea of citizenship in the kingdom and how to live in the kingdom. Use other passages to show the shape of the kingdom. Show how Jesus healed people (Mark 5), restored hope, and mended broken relationships. Be sure to stress that the kingdom has not yet come in all its fullness and that we must live in a broken world where redemption and healing is still in process. We need to pray continually, "Thy kingdom come." Preach a series on the parables of the kingdom and bring out these points. When strife is placed in the setting of the kingdom, people will be able to process the conflict better; they will know what to expect in life and when to expect the final solutions to their traumas.

The Attributes of God

Preaching on the attributes of God points to God as the source of help. This engenders hope. Think of what God's faithfulness, patience, love, and forgiving grace can mean to a hurting congregation. Actually it is only in the light of who God is and what he does that any healing takes place. When the reality of God's grace grips the souls of our people, there will be a change in attitude. No wonder John wrote, "Whoever does not love does not know God because God is love" and "Whoever loves God must also love his brother" (1 John 4:8, 21).

The Covenant

Covenant involves relationships. Palmer Robertson writes,

> By the very act of creating man in His own likeness and image, God established a unique relationship between Himself and creation. In addition to this sovereign creation-act, God spoke to man, thus determining precisely the role of man in creation. Through this creating/speaking relationship, God established sovereignly a life-and-death bond. This original bond between God and man may be called the covenant of creation.[3]

The Old Testament is the story of Israel's covenant life with God and each other. They frequently broke covenant with him and one another. The same thing is true of the strife-torn church. Preaching about Israel's covenant breaking and God's forgiving grace enables people to understand the kind of God they have: One who will reestablish covenant with them, build a covenant life with them, and heal the hurts from broken covenants. Properly preaching the promises of the covenant should bring great encouragement to a dispirited congregation. Hearing the conditions of the covenant should challenge them to obedience. Sermons on God's faithfulness, patience, and long-suffering help people see how God handles relationships. Preach through the book of Hosea or trace the covenant relationship of God with his people through the Old Testament. In the light of God's covenant keeping with them, our people will be able to understand keeping covenant with each other.

Selections of Scripture

Consider preaching through a book or large segment of the Bible. Those suggested in my survey as particularly appropriate are as follows:

> The Book of Ephesians (The Church, Christ's Body)
> The Book of Joshua (Claiming God's Promises)
> 1 Corinthians 13 (Love)
> Selections of the Life of Christ
> The Beatitudes
> The Sermon on the Mount
> Ephesians 6 (Christian Warfare)
> Galatians 5 (The Fruit of the Spirit)
> 1 Corinthians 12 (Spiritual Gifts)
> Ezra or Nehemiah
> 1 Peter (The Epistle of Hope)
> Romans 8 (Assurance)
> Philippians 2 (Humility)
> Revelation 2–3 (Is This My Church?)
> The Lord's Prayer
> 1 John (How to Experience Fellowship)
> Ezekiel (Prophecy of Hope)
> James (Living Our Faith)

Pastors found these portions of Scripture helpful in preaching to a divided church. Additional subjects mentioned were witnessing, Christ's identification with our difficulties, looking toward the future, grace, sanctification, love of brother, our responsibilities to God, the love of God, self-sacrifice, forgiveness, reconciliation, and cross-bearing. We should not find it difficult to apply these topics to the dilemma in our churches.

This chapter tries to demonstrate the necessity of a positive thrust in the content of our preaching. Concentrating on the nature of God opens the door to a bigger room of hope for the believer feeling claustrophobic in the conflict. Positive content is prerequisite to preaching that heals.

So is a positive attitude. The preacher needs to exhibit the hope that he has in a God who is bigger than the troubles of the moment. Often this seems impossible to a preacher as he watches his church fall apart. How to develop and maintain a positive outlook is discussed in the next chapter.

8

Positive Preaching

The strife-torn congregation needs to hear preaching that is positive, encouraging, and uplifting. Often the people can see only their battle scars; they have no vision for peace. We can give them that vision. Moving the church toward that positive goal will not be easy. Negativity seems to breed more negativity. How can we obtain what God desires for us?

How, indeed, can anything positive be accomplished? An obvious place to start is to examine our preaching. I asked pastors of strife-torn churches the following question: "What did you find most helpful in your preaching: emphasizing the congregation's strengths, weaknesses, both, neither, or other?" The unanimous reply was stressing the strengths, not the weaknesses. No one believed that stressing the weaknesses would aid the healing of the conflict, although twenty percent replied they preached about both the strengths and weaknesses. Another twenty percent marked the "other" slot on the questionnaire with remarks such as these:

> "I projected an image of what the church could become"
> "Emphasis on the Great Commission"
> "Emphasizing the adequacy of Christ to pull us together"
> "Keeping the preaching honest, but encouraging and helpful"
> "Giving them a vision beyond themselves"
> "Emphasizing what we are in Christ"

Positive preaching, then, is essential. But such preaching cannot spring from a vacuum. A positive attitude needs to exist, exhibited in both actions and words. How can we develop such a positive attitude? What can this do for the church?

A Positive Attitude

How can we remain positive when everything is negative? "It is all too easy in the midst of conflict to lose perspective, to see only the negative, to overlook whatever positive elements there may be in the situation."[1] H. Beecher Hicks, Jr. says he remained positive by maintaining healthy relationships with those in the congregation who could affirm, support, and be loyal to him. Personally, I concentrate on who they are in Christ. Whether a person is obnoxious or cantankerous, he is still in Christ. I must love him. If God loves the sinner, should I not do the same (Matt. 18:33)? As shepherd of the flock, learn to inwardly and lovingly embrace all the people whether they support you or not. Such a positive attitude will affect your approach to preaching. See the potential, possibilities, and calling God has for each person.

Paul could have dismissed the Corinthian church as a complete failure. Divisions, internal conflicts, jealousy, and quarreling might have led him to conclude, "This church isn't worth further effort and attention. Why bother with a group of people so weak, unloving, and stubborn?" Is that how you feel about your church?

Paul's attitude, however, is very positive. He tells the Corinthians they are "sanctified in Christ Jesus and called to be holy" (1 Cor. 1:2). He is thankful for them because of God's grace in their lives (1:4). He repeatedly calls them his brothers in Christ (1:10–11, 26; 2:1; 3:1), his dear children (4:14), whom he loves much: "My love to all of you in Christ Jesus" (16:24). Throughout, he demonstrates sincere feeling and concern. He teaches, admonishes, appeals, and pleads for them to become a healthy church.

The letter's optimism, encouragement, and hope indicate Paul took a positive attitude toward the troubled Corinthians: "You are God's people." Our attitude should be the same. Preaching in a strife-torn church requires visualizing the potential and possibilities of what God can do. We must truly believe that God can heal our torn and fractured church. Dissension and disruption need not continue. Our confidence in God will profoundly influence our preaching, which in turn will influence the congregation.

A colleague came to a church that had experienced a mass exodus of members. Only a few old people and several young couples remained. There were but two children. If any church appeared hopeless, this one did. But the pastor had faith that God could bring this church to life. God used prayer, preaching, and pastoral work to bring new families. In five years there were more than fifty children. The pastor believed God had a plan and purpose for this church. He took a positive attitude in the rebuilding process. I went to listen to him preach and discovered realistic optimism and hope. He offered a vision of God's purpose for his people.

Strengths and Weaknesses

Stress both the strengths and weaknesses of the church. Paul did. He tells the Corinthians that they lack no spiritual gifts (1 Cor. 1:7), they are Christians (1:9), and God's grace has enriched them in every way (1:5). He holds before them the positive qualities of their faith and riches in Christ.

Paul also reminds them of imperfections. His purpose in writing is to resolve the internal strife so they could become a strong witness in the city. Paul neither exaggerates nor overreacts. In approaching issue after issue he maintains a firm but sensitive approach to their problems.

How do we keep a balance? One pastor wrote me that we ought to be "lifting up the strengths, celebrating the successes, being very *gentle* about the weaknesses." Faults must not be ignored; sidestepping the defects does not solve them. Paul did not give a generic message to fit all situations, but addressed specific, sensitive issues. This brought positive results. As we touch the raw nerves of conflict, we must do so with a positive, redemptive thrust. When we talk about the blemishes, we are to do so with inner pain, understanding, and biblical solutions. Stressing only the strengths or weaknesses will promote unrealistic views. Honesty and healing demand both.

How much should we stress one or the other? That depends on each situation. How serious and damaging is the weakness? How obvious are the strengths? Paul uses considerable space to deal with the divisions in Corinth, yet writes only a few verses to address the lawsuits members had with each other. Looking at the book as a whole, it is clear that Paul spends more time discussing weaknesses than strengths. But he does so redemptively—in hope of change.

Paul judged each church and wrote accordingly. The Philippians received praise with little rebuke. In addressing the seven churches in Asia Minor (Rev. 2–3), Christ gave an honest evaluation of both the virtues and the vices of those churches. We should do the same in our preaching. Christian wisdom and the nature of the conflict must dictate the balance.

Preaching Hope

The Preacher's Hope

To preach positively is to preach hope to a people who feel caught in a futile struggle. To preach hope, we must be full of hope (1 Tim. 1:1). This hope in Christ gives us peace with God, ourselves, and others. Christ our hope enables us to be hopeful and optimistic. The congregation must see in us a model of joy, assurance, confidence, and security. Hope is the "anchor for the soul, firm, and secure" (Heb. 6:19). This makes us less defensive (a problem many ministers have), more relaxed, able to take both constructive and destructive criticism without overreacting. It makes us calm and positive about the conflict and hopeful about the future.

Paul would not have written the letter to the Corinthians unless he was optimistic about their recovery. He expressed that very thought in his second letter: "I wrote as I did so that when I came I should not be distressed by those who ought to make me rejoice. I had confidence in all of you, that you would all share my joy" (2 Cor. 2:3). Paul had confidence in the power of God to produce change in the lives of warring people. He also believed the Corinthians would respond to the challenge to change. Our churches will sense our optimism; they will be even quicker to sense a pessimistic and spiritless attitude.

Preach the Promises of God

Build hope by preaching on the promises of God. The Bible is filled with promises from cover to cover. When internal conflict plagued the Israelites, God made promises to them. When they were weary and despairing, God sent prophets to speak words of hope. Ezekiel saw the nation as a valley of dry dead bones, but God showed him that the bones could live (Ezek. 37). God forgave them and promised a future filled with blessing: "Comfort, comfort my people, says your God. Speak tenderly to Jerusalem, and proclaim to her that her hard service [strife] has been completed, that her sin has been paid for" (Isa. 40:1–2).

A friend recently polled my congregation to assess their hopefulness. He asked whether they struggled with discouragement, depression, or despair. Forty percent said "very little," another forty percent said "little," but twenty percent replied "much." If this exists in a healthy church without debilitating strife, imagine the percentage where conflict exists! The survey indicated that hopelessness most often occurs during times of loss, whether of health, possessions, or relationships. It also disclosed the need for more sermons on hope to obtain a clearer understanding of what hope is.

When the condition of a church seems desperate, nothing

inspires like a message on God's faithfulness. I have often used this theme to remind people that God is still in control, is the king, and has promised to abide with us. We can choose songs for worship that complement that theme, such as "Jesus With Your Church Abide," "Our God Reigns," "Rejoice, the Lord Is King," and "Great Is Thy Faithfulness." This will reinforce our message and bring hope to our people.

Jeremiah writes about the lamentable conditions of his time—of trouble, conflict, gloom, and grief—but he sparks a fire of hope when he says:

> I remember my affliction and my wandering, the bitterness and the gall. I well remember them, and my soul is cast down within me. Yet this I call to mind and therefore I have hope: Because of the Lord's great love we are not consumed, for his compassions never fail. They are new every morning; great is your faithfulness (Lam. 3:19–23).

God never abandons his work. "He who began a good work in you will carry it on to completion" (Phil. 1:6). Samuel Salter said,

> Every divine promise is built on four pillars: God's justice or holiness, which will not permit Him to deceive; His grace or goodness, which will not permit Him to forget; His truth, which will not permit Him to change; and His power, which makes Him able to accomplish.[2]

Preach God's promises to a strife-torn church. They desperately need these. They need to know that their God "is able to do immeasurably more than all we ask or imagine, according to his power that is at work within us" (Eph. 3:20).

Giving Hope

Ted came to an inner-city church declining in membership. As a young preacher he was expected to turn it around and attract young families. Most of the people were old and lived in a dangerous neighborhood around the church. Some wanted to relocate the church to the suburbs where several members lived. That is the point at which the tension began.

Some were opposed to any change, others saw a dying church. As the conflict continued, everyone became discouraged. It seemed hopeless. How could Ted keep a positive attitude in himself and the people he served? He did several things.

Rather than condemning some for abandoning the neighborhood or being stubborn about not relocating, Ted kept a positive message before his people. He did this by celebrating what the church had been and is. When he preached on "Ebenezer" (1 Sam. 7:12), he pointed to what God had done in the past and reminded the people that the Lord of the past is also the Lord of the future. Ted was building hope.

Ted also preached on Isaiah 51:1—"Look to the rock from which you were cut, and to the quarry from which you were hewn"—on the anniversary of the founding of the church. He spoke of the church as reaching back to the time of Abraham (Isa. 51:2) and how from one individual God had built a great nation. He emphasized the miracle of it all. Then he placed the congregation in that tradition and spoke of the continuity of God's plan. He pointed to all the sons and daughters who were baptized, confirmed, and married in that church building. He did not view it as a declining congregation, but as one that had served well through its history. This brought hope to the listeners. They began to feel good about their church.

Another of Ted's sermon texts was 1 Timothy 3:15: "If I am delayed, you will know how people ought to conduct themselves in God's household, which is the church of the living God, the pillar and foundation of the truth." Ted reminded his church that it had been a pillar supporting the infallible truth of Scripture. He related how that truth was embraced by the church's founders and how the congregation had been faithful through the years.

Ted kept preaching about the ministry of the congregation, what it had done, what it could do, the challenge of being a servant, and how to meet the needs of the world.

What the people did not immediately realize was that Pastor Ted was *reshaping the issue*. He was implying that location of ministry was not as important as ministry itself. True, decisions had to be made, but this was done in the context of a positive image of God's sovereign purpose of the church.

Pastor Ted could have taken a negative approach, scolding the people, promoting one side of the issue, alienating the rest of the congregation, and creating friction. But he didn't. The congregation finally decided to remain where it was to serve the community by instituting new ministries for the neighborhood. Young professional people soon began to join the congregation, although others left for suburban churches. The church went through a transformation rather peacefully because the positive preaching of hope facilitated that change.

Preaching Purpose

Another way to create a positive outlook is to preach about the church's purpose. Challenge the body of Christ to a new vision of God's will for them. The congregation should honestly face the question, "Why do we exist?" Answer that question through preaching. Here are some ways to do that.

The Church Serves the Kingdom

Study the relationship of the church to the kingdom. According to Howard Snyder, "The Bible is full of teaching on the kingdom of God, and the church has largely missed it. The kingdom of God is a key thread in Scripture, tying the whole Bible together."[3] One purpose of the church is to advance the interests of the kingdom of God. The church prays, "Thy kingdom come," then works to bring about the reality of the kingdom here and now. True, there is a future dimension to the kingdom, but the purpose of the church is to build the kingdom now.

To do this the church must evangelize. That is how God brings people into his kingdom. Then the church must train and disciple these new citizens of the kingdom (Matt. 28:20;

1 Tim. 4:13). Further, members of the church are to worship, fellowship, and give. Preaching must motivate and energize Christians to transform the world. This is how the kingdom comes.

I have found that preaching the kingdom of God gives people a broad biblical vision of the church's duties. One's church is not an end in itself; it serves a higher purpose. In a series of sermons I traced the concept of the kingdom of God through Scripture. This was profitable in that it gave a new sense of purpose to our congregation. Is your church hindering or advancing the kingdom? Our preaching should emphasize how important God considers the kingdom to be and whether the congregation's conflict is hindering or advancing it.[4]

Facing Contemporary Issues Positively

Perhaps our church is not ready for a theology of the kingdom. Then develop the purpose of the church through preaching on specific issues. Suppose we preach on abortion, encouraging our members to pray for the unborn, support the local pregnancy crisis center, and open their homes to unwed mothers. Our church could become a center for the pro-life movement as we shape the people's thinking through preaching. We should not use contemporary issues to cover up or ignore the conflict, but to get at the purpose of the church. Preach the biblical response to problems such as world hunger, euthanasia, suicide, racism, wealth, war, and sex. Show how your church can be involved in the solutions. This will give a positive thrust to your ministry.

I once heard a minister speak on these issues in a devastatingly negative manner. The world was depicted in such a state of decay that any attempt to rectify it seemed hopeless. What effect do you suppose this would have on an already demoralized church? Be positive!

Most controversies can be approached from a positive angle. My denomination has a special day each year to celebrate the diverse ethnic groups in the church. On such an occasion, rather than condemn racism, celebrate the variety of races in Christ's body. Preach a sermon on unity between Jews and Gentiles in Christ (Eph. 2). Preach on poverty and hunger, and involve the church with a specific, needy family or sponsor a refugee family. Point toward the purpose of the church *through sermons that call for action.*

We can show our people that a dispute about the color of the choir robes, remodeling the women's restroom, removing some ancient landmark like the outdoor bulletin board erected in memory of a long-deceased member, or the pastor's wardrobe is irrelevant to the purpose of the church. Often church conflict stems from insignificant matters like these. Preaching issues can keep a vision before people that will not allow them the myopic view of thinking the church exists only to perpetuate itself.

Paul directed the attention of the controversy-riddled Corinthian church toward practical Christian living. "Always give yourselves fully to the work of the Lord" (1 Cor. 15:58). Don't quibble among yourselves, but give generously to the needy in Jerusalem (16:1–4). Express love among yourselves (chap. 13), worship in an orderly manner (14:40), use your spiritual gifts for others (12:7), eat and drink to the glory of God (10:31).

Have you defined the purpose of your church? Do your people know what that purpose is? If not, that may be the source of the conflict.

But conflict does not always result from a congregation's lack of understanding of its purpose. Division also occurs because false doctrine, immorality, or offensive behavior exists. Preaching in such a scenario is the topic of the next chapter.

9

Prudent Preaching

Addressing the moral issues of your church requires prudent preaching—preaching that is well-reasoned, discreet, and wise. It is preaching that displays a discerning and discriminating approach to strife. The need for such preaching is found in the fact that conflict is usually filled with emotion. Feelings run high and reason does not always prevail. As people become involved in conflict, they often become irrational. The church becomes a tinderbox ready to catch fire, a time bomb ready to explode at the slightest jostling. Preaching in such a church requires wisdom and prudence. It takes sensitivity on the one hand and firmness on the other.

A pastor in southern California was very evangelistic. Every sermon consisted of a simple presentation of the gospel, and the congregation had grown weary of the repetition. They wanted instruction, discipleship, the meat of the Word, growth-oriented sermons. The pastor did not change his method and after a few years was separated from his congregation, another casualty of conflict. Had he been prudent, he would have balanced his preaching. He would have prevented conflict rather than producing it.

Addressing Immoral Behavior Prudently

My neighbor and colleague was an alcoholic. Although confronted by various people, including his church council, he refused help. Many Sundays he was unable to preach until, finally, he was suspended from his office. The Sunday after it happened, I was asked to preach in that church. What was prudent? Should I ignore the problem and preach on the Second Coming? Should I face the issue that was dividing the church? If so, what should I say? What would you have done?

I chose as my text Galatians 6:1–5:

> Brothers, if someone is caught in a sin, you who are spiritual should restore him gently. But watch yourself or you may be tempted. Carry each other's burdens, and in this way you will fulfill the law of Christ. If anyone thinks he is something when he is nothing, he deceives himself. Each one should test his own actions. Then he can take pride in himself, without comparing himself to somebody else, for each one should carry his own load.

I spoke of how alcoholism includes a heavy load of guilt. I urged the brother to seek help as well as God's forgiveness. To a certain point the brother had to carry his own load; no one could do it for him. He alone could assume responsibility for his actions and behavior. At the same time, I urged the congregation to help him carry his load. They were to be nonjudgmental, look to their own failures, and be humble, compassionate, and forgiving. The sermon placed responsibility on *everyone* for the healing of the church.

The response to this sermon was overwhelming. The congregation became open and gentle to their pastor. Unfortunately, he did not conquer his fault or confess his sin, and he was eventually dismissed from the ministry. But the church recovered rapidly. The sermon set the stage for recovery, not by producing more trauma but by prudently approaching the problem.

In 1 Corinthians 5, Paul confronted a delicate moral problem that the church in Corinth was ignoring. "It is actually reported that there is sexual immorality among you, and of a kind that does not occur even among pagans: A man has his father's wife" (v. 1). Paul displayed an unflinching approach to sin, yet a serious concern for the welfare of the entire congregation. He didn't hesitate to address sin and to recommend what to do about it: "Expel the wicked man from among you" (v. 13). Paul was concerned about the potential damage this particular problem might cause: "Don't you know that a little yeast works through the whole batch of dough?" (v. 6). Other problems in the church such as quarreling, lawsuits, jealousy, pride, and selfishness did not warrant such radical discipline. Paul addressed each issue individually, with directness and sensitivity, elsewhere in his letter to the church.

Preaching is a form of discipline. John Calvin wrote,

> If no society, even no home, though containing only a small family, can be preserved in a proper state without discipline, this is far more necessary in the church, the state of which ought to be the most orderly of all. As the saving doctrine of Christ is the soul of the church, so discipline forms the ligaments which connect the members together, and keep each in its proper place.[1]

Personal discipline at work, at home, in the community, and in the church is necessary for harmony and unity in those areas of life. Preaching is one way to administer that discipline. When Paul addresses the issues of worldliness, jealousy, quarreling, disputes, pride, etc., he is disciplining the people. Actually it is not so much Paul who disciplines, but God through his Word. This is one purpose of Scripture: "All Scripture is God breathed and is useful for teaching, rebuking, correcting, and training in righteousness, so that the man of God may be thoroughly equipped for every good work" (2 Tim. 3:16–17).

If something is occurring in your church that is a clear violation of the will of God, the discipline of the Scriptures through preaching should be applied. After all, such behavior destroys the unity of the body and should not be tolerated. True, there will be pastoral counseling and visits, but preaching ought not be neglected. God's Word is powerful; "living and active, sharper than any double-edged sword, it penetrates even to dividing soul and spirit, joints and marrow;

it judges the thoughts and attitudes of the heart" (Heb. 4:12). This Word prudently preached in the heat of a church fight may change sinful behavior into godly behavior.

Addressing False Doctrine Prudently

Doctrinal contention undoubtedly is one of the worst kind. Everyone involved is convinced he is on God's side defending the church against heresy. When orthodoxy is perceived to be at stake, the fight may become vile. People forget that adherence to right doctrine is equally important to adherence to right behavior. Often the fruit of the Spirit is sacrificed on the altar of truth.

In all denominations there is a certain amount of controversy swirling around. The issues may include the inerrancy of Scripture, ordination of women or homosexuals, the doctrine of the Holy Spirit, spiritual gifts, or eschatology. The official denominational publications contain articles on these controversial issues, and the people are drawn into the debates. We sense some people leaning one way, others the opposite direction. Soon the terms "liberal" and "conservative" are voiced. Groups form to promote their viewpoint, and tension mounts each month. Speakers fuel the fire on both sides, and the debate heats up. Some demand the "liberals" get out; others accuse the "conservatives" of being close-minded. There is talk about splitting the church.

We have come to preach in this church. How will we handle the situation? Will we identify with the group that satisfies our personal inclinations and justify it with the declaration "but that's the truth!"? What would be the *prudent* thing to do?

First, determine the weightiness of the issue. Some doctrines lie at the heart and essence of Christianity, others at the periphery. The historic church has spoken in councils and creeds on some of the central doctrines. If the dispute centers on such cardinal teachings as the inspiration of Scripture, the deity of Christ, salvation by grace alone through faith, the Trinity, the second coming of Christ, or like topics, preach to inform and to instruct in a convincing manner so that the Scripture's teaching is crystal clear to everyone.

Some doctrines, such as the Millennium, do not carry the same weight. Our preaching should not major on the minor doctrines. This does not mean ignoring the Millennium in preaching, but if it is the cause of conflict in our church, we should place this doctrine in proper perspective to all other doctrines. Our preaching itself can lead people to understand what issues are important. We show them by our choice of themes which doctrines are central. If we repeatedly preach the doctrine of the last things, the congregation will consider that truth worth fighting about, even to the point of splitting the church. Prudent preachers know where to draw the battle lines. Do we?

Second, even when an important doctrine is at stake, prudence requires a style of preaching that does not inflame or incite. A minister recently preached a sermon on Genesis 2:7, the creation of man, accusing and condemning specific Christian scientists of not being Christians. True or not, this approach to preaching is likely to divide a church. In fact, the church where this minister serves is already taking sides. A wise preacher will ask how this subject may be preached in a way that unites the body in the truth. Inform the people; but be cautious. The doctrine of origins is important, but the Christian community is not agreed on the *how* of creation. In our preaching we must show respect to those who seriously grapple with current issues. We must be positive and present our insights as best we can without degrading, slandering, or casting aspersions on someone who disagrees with us. This is the prudent way.

Early in my ministry I thought I ought to expose all the differences in doctrine between me and other communions. I have since learned to be much more prudent about those differences. We should ask who our brothers and sisters in Christ are, and preach so our people will place doctrinal matters and differences in proper perspective. Wisdom dictates that we not be too dogmatic on matters not specifically addressed in Scripture. My father and mother are premillenarian, but I am amillenarian. This doctrinal difference in no way hinders or interferes with our relationships. Let all our preaching show that kind of prudence.

The Corinthians not only engaged in immoral behavior, but embraced false doctrine. Some in Corinth believed in the resurrection of the body, others did not (1 Cor. 15:12). Unless there is unity in essential doctrines, trauma will continue. In 1 Corinthians 15, Paul makes a dramatic case for the doctrine of our bodily resurrection. It settled the differences. Preaching the essential truths of the Christian faith clearly and prudently contributes to the healing of the church. Those who refuse to accept these doctrines show that they are not a part of the body of Christ (1 John 2:19–20). Prudent preaching doesn't allow people to remain delinquent in behavior or belief, but approaches the differences with discernment.

The closer we all are to the Scriptures in doctrinal faithfulness, the closer we are to each other. Churches with confessional standards experience unity as the truths of those standards are preached. Churches with denominational affiliation have teachings that draw them together. Independent churches have unity in proportion to the doctrinal truths they hold in common. As pastors we must work hard to discipline ourselves in the Word, then let the Word discipline our people for true unity and healing to occur.

Preaching Tolerance Prudently

Allowing Diversity in Unity

Church conflict does not always erupt over issues that are clearly right or wrong. Often there are matters of opinion and judgment; no immorality is involved, and no doctrine is violated. One group wants certain things and demands that everyone else follow suit. The occasion might be the remodeling or relocation of the church building, the purchase of a new organ, or a change in the style of worship. I use puppets to present a children's message, and this upsets some people. Causes of church trauma are numerous and often begin as small, insignificant disagreements. The color of the drapes, the format of the bulletin, the arrangement of the flowers, or the appointment of a new janitor—all may precipitate trouble.

Does preaching have anything to say to these irritating, annoying experiences? Does the Bible give any guidelines in handling people's frustrations and peevishness? Most certainly. And our people must hear it from the pulpit!

Paul discovered people in Corinth (and our churches have them too) who are easily offended. In 1 Corinthians 8 he describes them as people with a weak conscience (v. 7). He instructs those who are offended by others eating meat sacrificed to idols that "an idol is nothing at all in the world" (v. 4). He tells them, "Food does not bring us near to God, we are no worse if we do not eat, and no better if we do" (v. 8). At the same time he instructs those who eat meat sacrificed to idols, "Be careful that the exercise of your freedom does not become a stumbling block to the weak" (v. 9). What Paul is promoting is tolerance in allowing diversity while maintaining unity.

The apostle has a similar message in regard to the matter of spiritual gifts. Trauma in Corinth arose when one group insisted their spiritual gifts exceeded those of others. Paul promotes unity by allowing diversity: "There are different kinds of gifts, but the same Spirit. There are different kinds of service, but the same Lord. There are different kinds of working, but the same God works all of them in all men. Now to each one the manifestation of the Spirit is given for the common good" (1 Cor. 12:4–7). Later he uses the figure of the human body to depict the unity and diversity in the church, showing that unity exists only when all the parts function together in diversity (1 Cor. 12).

I have averted potential conflict on specific occasions by preaching the beauty of diversity in unity. My church and denomination were not untouched by the charismatic movement in the sixties. Some pastors I knew preached against such phenomena as speaking in tongues. I saw tension rise in those churches; people became agitated, upset, even angry. I, too, needed to address this issue and answer people's questions. So I preached a series of sermons on the work of the Holy Spirit. I did so, however, allowing for the expression of different gifts as Paul advises in 1 Corinthians 12. The church I was serving never went through "the charismatic crisis."

Tension mounts when either diversity or unity is stressed to the exclusion of the other. Too much emphasis on diversity, freedom, and cultivation of an independent spirit leads to conflict because everyone wants to run the church according to his style. Too much stress on unity with no allowance for the diversity of gifts will make people feel disenfranchised with no outlet for their ideas. They will become discouraged, withdrawn, or contentious.

The Solution to Differences

The solution to the problem of differences lies in acknowledging the gifts of people, stressing that they are to be used for the body, not self. Show that, although each individual is important, no one is an end in himself; the body must profit from what God has given to each for the benefit of all.

Recognize the individual's conscience, but remember that it is not the standard to follow. Preach the cause as greater than any individual. Communicate that respect, tolerance, and affirmation are vital in our differences. Prudent preaching is discreet, wise, well-reasoned in getting people to accept diversity in the nonessentials of the church's life and to recognize others' varying gifts. Take care to distinguish essentials from adiaphora.[2] "Christian liberty teaches us that we are bound by no obligation before God respecting external things, which in themselves are indifferent."[3] Here is a specific example to flesh out the principle.

A certain church had instituted a "family night" program.

On Wednesday evening the entire congregation, from the babies in the nursery to adults, were invited to come for a meal prepared and served at minimal cost, after which children, youth groups, and adults gathered separately for Bible study and fellowship. It is neither right nor wrong (neither forbidden nor required) to have a family-night program but a few people adamantly opposed it. At the time I became pastor of that church, the family night was a source of growing friction, but when I left some years later, only a couple of people remained opposed. How did I handle this situation?

Had I preached that family night was a requirement for everyone, that this program was endorsed and instituted by the council of the church, and that everyone was duty-bound to attend, tension would have escalated. Instead, in my preaching I acknowledged the right of people not to attend, to form other groups for Bible study and fellowship, and to choose alternative ways to be involved in the church. As time passed, people became more tolerant and accepting of others' viewpoints. According to a survey conducted in the church some time later, this kind of preaching had assisted in bringing unity. I used passages such as Romans 12, 1 Corinthians 12, and Ephesians 4 to stress the importance of each person in the body of Christ and how each is to serve and to work for the entire body in a harmonious way.

Prudent preaching allows for legitimate differences of viewpoint, emphasis, and opinion. We should encourage these kinds of differences, or our churches will stagnate. Differences bring creativity, stimulate thought, and unleash fresh ideas. If we are dogmatic on every issue, answer every question, and claim authority on every subject, either the church will grow stale or conflict will increase. Prudent preaching draws lines carefully, biblically distinguishing what are adiaphora and what are not. Such preaching shows room for differences about the adiaphora and makes clear that these are matters for discussion, not for conflict.

Prudent preaching also submerges our differences in the

nonessentials and encourages members to join hands in doing the essential work of the Lord. We must not allow someone whose opinion is not followed to create conflict and destroy the unity of the church. Point people to the God we serve. Preach what the Bible says about servanthood and urge the congregation to subordinate personal agendas (including your own) to God's agenda for the body of which they are members. This is what membership in the church of Christ entails. Through preaching, create an atmosphere where "if one part suffers, every part suffers with it; if one part is honored, every part rejoices with it" (1 Cor. 12:26).

Let's assume that we weather the storm within our church. How do we know it is the end of the storm and not the eye of it? When can we consider our church healthy? The final chapter will help us identify the marks of recovery and maturity.

10

Recovery Through Preaching

Wounded churches can heal. Scars diminish until there is barely a trace of the conflict. This recovery period is actually a time of maturing. Healing, maturing, and growth are different ways of describing the same process. Recovery as a process can be enhanced through preaching.

There are many elements in this process. Let's identify the ways in which preaching facilitates it.

The Road to Recovery

The Grief Process

The strife-torn church grieves because it experiences loss. One church I came to serve had lost membership and both its pastors. Some of the congregation were relieved by this, others were greatly distressed. There was a loss of unity, harmony, and closeness. Strife brings a loss of joy, peace, vision, excitement, and even ministry. Churches lose their pride and esprit de corps. Their honor, enthusiasm, and devotion vanish. Some even lose their property in court battles—one church I know was literally locked out of its building by the police. Other losses occur when conflict separates parents and children or relatives. Such serious and often lasting losses bring profound grief.

Some people cope by denying the grief: "Our church is

good, we don't have any problems, everything is just fine." Regarding my own congregation, I actually had a person tell me, "Pastor, our problems were all solved in a couple of weeks, even before you arrived." It is difficult for a church to admit it has problems; people want to believe their church is the best in town. They don't want to face the harsh reality of conflict or their weaknesses and losses.

Growth and change are both difficult. It is much easier to engage in denial. The Pharisees felt no need to change, the Corinthians were smug about their quarreling, and the Laodicean church was verbally taken to task, "You say, 'I am rich; I have acquired wealth and do not need a thing.' But you do not realize that you are wretched, pitiful, poor, blind, and naked'" (Rev. 3:17). All those groups lost a vital relationship with God but denied it.

Our church may even think fighting is normal. Some churches seem to be in constant turmoil. These churches remind me of a young couple I know who began their marriage in conflict because the husband grew up in a family where there was continual yelling and arguing. The wife was reared in a home where she never witnessed even a cross word between her parents. The honeymoon was a disaster, because the husband began arguing and the wife could not understand why this was happening. Does our church understand the dynamics of a church fight? Do we? Check out the responses to grief.

Losses are frequently accompanied with anger. Grief may express itself in anger. We as pastors may be the target of unreasonable ire. I have often felt like a pincushion as people unloaded their anger on me. They will blame us as pastors for getting them into this mess or for not getting them out of it.

Or they will withhold their contributions. My church fell several thousand dollars in arrears after the conflict developed. Attendance decreased, an uncooperative attitude evolved, people began to find scapegoats, resignations occurred, and blame was bandied about. Grief brings strange reactions.

Have you noticed how sad you feel when you lose

something? No one is really happy about the trouble. A pall of pessimism hangs over the congregation. There are doubts about the future. Discouragement permeates the church, and no one wants to invest himself in this plight. Even the loyalists want to give up.

Are we aware of these attitudes? Will we allow the church to go through its grief? Don't be in too much of a hurry to eradicate the pain. If we brush it aside, latent anger and resentment may surface later. Preach comfort and hope, pointing to Christ who never forsakes his own (Heb. 13:5). Guide people into letting go of the past. Use Philippians 3:13: "But one thing I do: Forgetting what is behind and straining toward what is ahead, I press on toward the goal to win the prize for which God has called me heavenward in Christ Jesus." Preach in a way that acknowledges anger, grief, and loss as real, but that also sees problems as a means to maturity as the body considers "everything a loss compared to the surpassing greatness of knowing Christ Jesus" (Phil. 3:8).

The Maturing Process

One sermon will not heal a church. Neither will a short stay of a month or two. Churches mature slowly and need much time to grow. Philippians 2:1–18 indicates how such growth occurs. The chapter opens with Paul urging harmony. This harmony is based on union with Christ, the encouragement of his love, and a fellowship through the Holy Spirit; these foundations make the people capable of tenderness and compassion (vv. 1–4). Paul presents an example of the sort of humility that leads to harmony—the incarnation and death of Jesus Christ (vv. 5–11). Having identified the basis for unity and an example of the attitude that facilitates it, he now draws a conclusion: "Continue to work out your salvation with fear and trembling, for it is God who works in you to will and to act according to his good purpose" (vv. 12–13).

Paul does not urge his readers to work *for* their salvation, but to work *out* their salvation. In this context, salvation is growth, maturity, problem solving, and developing the mind of Christ. The catalyst for this growth is our status in Christ (vv. 1–4), exemplified in the example of Christ, that now becomes the responsibility of each person. Growth comes through working out our salvation. This means "no complaining or arguing," being "blameless and pure, children of God without fault in a crooked and depraved generation," and shining "like stars in the universe, as you hold out the word of life" (vv. 14–16).

Maturity comes through consistent, strenuous effort. The incentive is God in you enabling you to will and act according to his good purpose. The Corinthian church, according to Paul, was immature, "mere infants in Christ" (1 Cor. 3:1). Spiritual infancy has little to do with chronological age, but much to do with attitudes and behavior. Jealousy and quarreling indicate spiritual infancy (1 Cor. 3:3). If there is much of this in our church, we must conclude it is immature. Challenge the people in your preaching to work out their problems (their salvation) and to grow into maturity. Hold before the people the qualities that demonstrate mature thought and action (1 Peter 2:1–3). Hold up to them Jesus Christ, the epitome of perfection.

Be aware that maturity is a process. It takes time to change. Growth comes slowly through effort and prayer. Not all want to make that kind of investment in the conflict. For their own reasons they want to keep the conflict alive.

Remain with the church for the amount of time it takes for maturity to take place. I stayed in a strife-torn church eleven years. It would have been a mistake to leave after four or five. Short pastorates usually do not result in great growth and maturity. God is never in a hurry, nor are there spiritual vitamins to dispense for speedy growth. The maturing process depends on the willingness of a church to change its behavior as the Holy Spirit works in soil receptive to growth.

The Marks of Personal Maturity

Church maturity begins with personal maturity. What do we look for in personal maturity? Various lists are given in

Scripture, and Philippians 4:8 is one such list: "Whatever is true, whatever is noble, whatever is right, whatever is pure, whatever is lovely, whatever is admirable—if anything is excellent or praiseworthy—think about such things." The fruit of the Spirit (Gal. 5:22–26) also gauges maturity. A list especially appropriate for a strife-torn church is found in James 3:17: "But the wisdom that comes from heaven is first of all pure; then peace-loving, considerate, submissive, full of mercy and good fruit, impartial and sincere."

Heavenly wisdom is pure. If our people possess this wisdom, they will be free from jealousy, selfishness, and personal ambition. Purity here means to be single-minded, not double-minded (James 1:7). Maturity has come when our people serve God sincerely, without desire for personal gain or ulterior motives. They are grown up when they serve their Lord out of the sheer delight of doing so: "Blessed are the pure in heart" (Matt. 5:8).

Look for a peace-loving spirit in the congregation. When our people love peace more than conflict, when they "make every effort to keep the unity of the Spirit through the bond of peace" (Eph. 4:3), they are showing maturity. To be spiritually full-grown is to delight in healing and restoring what is fractured. Do our people have a caring, unselfish, empathetic spirit? Are they cooperative and forgiving like God, the Great Forgiver and Reconciler?

Worldly wisdom is inconsiderate and therefore immature. It tramples on people and is boorish, ill-mannered, and insensitive to others. Heavenly wisdom is charitable, thoughtful, reasonable, and solicitous. Does this characterize our people? If so, they have become mature; if not, we should preach more about heavenly wisdom. Base the sermons on what God has done and is doing in Christ. Show that each of these characteristics belongs to him in perfection. Preach so that what people are asked to do is based on what God has already done for them in Christ. Tell them not to live contractually (by rules, contracts, legal documents, the letter of the law) but covenantally (by promises, grace, and forgiveness). That is how God deals with us.

Another trait of maturity is submissiveness. Do our people "submit to one another out of reverence for Christ" (Eph. 5:21)? Worldly wisdom is stubborn and opinionated. Maturity is open-minded, amenable to change, willing to listen, even willing to deny self. James refers to people who are teachable, good listeners, who profit from instruction. A self-willed person is not ordinarily submissive. When our church displays this mark of maturity, conflict will diminish.

Preach mercy, because people are unmerciful in a conflict. Church trauma produces many bruised and battered people. Jesus was merciful even to those who abused him. He is full of pity and asks us to be the same. Urge people to cultivate the tenderness of Jesus: "A bruised reed he will not break, and a smoldering wick he will not snuff out" (Isa. 42:3). Season your preaching with the spirit of mercy.

When good fruit appears on the tree of life, there is evidence of maturity. "This is to my Father's glory, that you bear much fruit, showing yourselves to be my disciples" (John 15:8). The fruit of righteousness (Phil. 1:11; Heb. 12:11; James 3:18), the fruit of repentance (Luke 3:8), and the fruit of good works flowing from a good heart (Matt. 12:33–37) are fruits of maturity.

A mature person is also impartial. James directed his words to those who show partiality to the rich at the expense of the poor:

> If you show special attention to the man wearing fine clothes and say, "Here's a good seat for you," but say to the poor man, "You stand there" or "Sit on the floor by my feet," have you not discriminated among yourselves and become judges with evil thoughts? (James 2:3–4).

In a church fight it is difficult to remain impartial. But the Lord shows no favoritism. Challenge the people to follow Christ and become mature.

James's list includes sincerity. Honesty and openness are often absent from a church conflict. People engage in power plays, cover-ups, half-truths, and slanted presentations. Everyone thinks of himself as sincerely right instead of as sincerely humble and repentant.

The mature person can deal with differences of opinion in a sincere, noncombative way. Preach a heavenly wisdom that enables people to understand another's viewpoint.

These are a few of the qualities of a mature person. Preaching them will focus on what people ought to be as they seek to have the mind of Christ. Our calling as a prophet is to preach until all "reach unity in the faith and in the knowledge of the Son of God and become mature attaining to the whole measure of the fullness of Christ" (Eph. 4:13). Personal maturity will directly affect how rapidly and completely our church will recover from trauma.

The Marks of a Healthy Church

When is a church fully recovered? Perhaps never. Perhaps to some degree. We can only approximate total health since the church exists in a broken world. Trauma may leave some people bitter for life, even though they are commanded to "get rid of all bitterness" (Eph. 4:31). Perfection will not be achieved in this life. Open recognition that we have not "already obtained all this, or have already been made perfect" (Phil. 3:12) is the best way to understand the limits of our recovery goal. Although perfection cannot be achieved, much can be accomplished. Consider these traits of a recovery.

Service Centered

Since I define a strife-torn church as one where the level of conflict has caused serious injury to the body, immobilizing it in its ministry and outreach, one of the marks of recovery is its ability to serve. The Corinthian church showed some signs of health when it gave gifts to the poor in Jerusalem (1 Cor. 16:1–4). The church that serves others beyond its own membership is a healthy church. It may serve through evangelism, missionary support programs, social action, or diaconal activity.

I have seen my church become interested in painting houses for the elderly and poor, collecting food, and encouraging families to be foster parents and to be involved in diaconal ministries. Budgets were met. Missionaries were supported at home and abroad. The church sent some of its members to the field. Two local churches were supported in a church-planting ministry. These are signs of health.

Recovery can also be seen in the service rendered to people within the church. Reaching out to the needy, hurting within the congregation—the unemployed, the depressed, the divorced, those with marital and personal problems—are signs of growth. Does our church have a servantlike attitude, empathy, and a desire to touch the lives of others? Our preaching can encourage a congregation to this kind of vigorous health.

Growth Oriented

Numerical and spiritual growth are signs of a robust church. Such a church welcomes new members, whether by evangelism, transfer, or commitment of its own children. A spirit of celebration, thanksgiving, and joy permeates the fellowship. My church became more deeply committed to prayer, small-group Bible study, education, and ministry to teens and children. It began a ministry to the mentally impaired. Other churches I know have initiated evangelism and ministries to substance abusers, singles, and street people. Signs of such activity show the church is growing.

Creative Energy

A church shows its maturity by how it handles new ideas. Does the church allow for creativity? Can it easily tolerate changes in worship, music, programming, and organization? Is the church easily threatened by some deviation from tradition? Is it afraid of failure? Is it willing to take risks? Do such things produce more trauma or a more meaningful church life? A mature church seeks to improve the quality of its corporate life, administrative techniques, educational programs, and communal worship. My church became innovative in its administrative structure, committed itself to a staffed youth ministry, remodeled the church building, continued its evangelism program, and expanded its diaconal outreach—all without further division! We will know the extent of recovery by how our church responds in these and other areas of service. Preach freedom and flexibility. Freedom is not doing what we want. It is doing what God wants, with joy and pleasure. Freedom is fulfilling our responsibility to others out of love and trust. "Keep reminding them of these things" (2 Tim. 2:14).

Positive Outlook

A healthy church is one with a positive outlook. The atmosphere is upbeat, and people are proud of their church. They talk about their church as if it were the best on earth. I visited a church recently that had received a new pastor. As I spoke with the parishioners, they were all appreciative of their pastor and congregation. "Wasn't that a great sermon!" "Our church is really friendly and we have a family spirit here." "Our pastor has a lot of great ideas." "Wasn't the music wonderful!" "I get the sermon tapes and listen to them during the week." The remarks went on and on. It isn't important how factual these statements are—that's not the point. They betray a spirit, a mood, a temper. These people loved their church and spoke positively about it. That is a healthy church.

Constant quarreling, complaining, and negativity are signs of sickness. Church members can see what is best in their brothers and sisters, or focus on their faults. Peter puts it this way: "Above all, love each other deeply, because love covers a multitude of sins" (1 Peter 4:8). And when our people live by 1 Corinthians 13:4–8, we have a healthy church.

United Spirit

The church is healthy when unity is restored. The scars of strife may remain, but the conflict no longer hinders the church's mission and ministry. Unity does not mean uniformity. Unity allows for diversity, but disallows divisions that hinder the progress and growth of the church. Paul's desire for the Corinthian church was "that all of you agree with one another so that there may be no divisions among you and that you may be perfectly united in mind and thought" (1 Cor. 1:10). Such a church will "keep the unity of the Spirit through the bond of peace" (Eph. 4:3).

The "mind" of the church needs to be one, not many. This must be evident in the belief system as well as in the intangible area of feeling, spirit, and purpose. There must be a unified spirit of cooperation in all the endeavors of the congregation. Whether a worship service or a church picnic, everyone participates. Unity comes when you "in humility consider others better than yourselves" (Phil. 2:3). The degree of unity is a barometer of the extent of health. We will observe recovery when votes are nearly unanimous, projects are undertaken enthusiastically, and worship is joyous and meaningful. Our church is recovered when praise replaces problems, peace supercedes protest, and relationships are restored. Preach until this happens!

Can it happen? As preachers we play a key role in a church's health. What is spoken from the pulpit has power as God employs the foolishness of preaching to save and heal those who believe (1 Cor. 1:21). Time and again God comes to his strife-torn world to bind up the brokenhearted. " 'I will restore you to health and heal your wounds,' declares the LORD" (Jer. 30:17). Preach in the confidence that this will occur in your church.

Appendix

Suggested Scripture passages and sermon titles to use in preaching to a strife-torn church.

Old Testament

Exodus 14:15: Moving On
Deuteronomy 7:6–16: God's Covenant Faithfulness
The book of Joshua: Claiming God's Promises
The book of 1 Samuel: Leadership Problems
2 Chronicles 33: God's Forgiveness
Job 31:35: Is Someone Listening?
Psalm 23: Personal Care
Psalm 51: Confession and Forgiveness
Psalm 103: Praise God
Psalm 121: God's Providence
Proverbs 15:1: Cool It!
Ecclesiastes 3: A Time for Everything
Isaiah 40:29–30: God Gives Strength
Isaiah 44:3–5: Streams in the Desert
Isaiah 53: Christ Identifies With Us
Isaiah 61: Good News
Jeremiah 29:8–14: God's Plan for You
Ezekiel 37:1–14: Can the Church Be Renewed?
Micah 7:18–20: When God Forgets

New Testament

The Sermon on the Mount
Matthew 5:1–13: God Believes in You
Matthew 5:9: Are You a Peacemaker?
Matthew 6:14–15: Forgiveness
Matthew 11:28–30: Rest for the Weary
Matthew 16:13–20: My Church Is Worthy Because . . .

Matthew 18:12–14: The Seeking Father
Matthew 18:21–22: The Limits of Forgiveness
Matthew 28:19–20: The Great Commission
Mark 5:1–19: Satan Will Use Us, If We Let Him
Luke 7:36–50: Critic or Lover
Luke 9:51–56: Misplaced Zeal
Luke 17:1–10: Forgiveness
The gospel of John: The Great I AM Passages
John 3:3: Born Again
John 4:4: Going Through Samaria: Turning
Difficulty Into Opportunity
John 13:34–35: They Will Know Us by Our Love
John 14: God's Presence Through Jesus Christ
John 15: Abiding in the Vine
John 17:15: Protection From Evil
John 17:20–26: A Prayer for Unity
John 20–21: Resurrection Hope
John 21:15–17: Not Tragedy But Triumph
The book of Acts: Christ Builds His Church
Acts 1:8: You Are My Witnesses
Acts 2:42–47: An Example of How to Achieve Unity
Acts 6:1–7: Church Problems
Acts 10:43: Living Expectantly
Acts 15: The Inclusive Church
Romans 5:1–5: Blessings in Christ
Romans 8: Security
Romans 8:31–39: We Are Not There Alone
Romans 12: Living Sacrifices
Romans 12:1–2, 9: Grateful Living
Romans 13:8–10: Loving Your Fellow Man
Romans 15:1–2: The Strong and the Weak
The book of 1 Corinthians: Moral and theological problems
1 Corinthians 1–4: Dealing With Conflict Redemptively
1 Corinthians 2:2: Creed and Deed
1 Corinthians 10:16–17: Participation in Christ
1 Corinthians 12: Unity and Diversity
1 Corinthians 13: The Ways of Love
1 Corinthians 14:40: Behaving Properly
The book of 2 Corinthians: Moral and theological problems
2 Corinthians 1:1–11: Comfort in Distress
2 Corinthians 5:15–6:1: God's Plan for Reconciliation Is Effective
Galatians 5:16–6:5: Living by the Spirit
Galatians 6: Bearing Burdens

The book of Ephesians
Ephesians 2: By God's Grace We Are What We Are
Ephesians 2:14–15: No More Hostility
Ephesians 4:11, 16: Building and Edifying
Ephesians 4:25–5:2: Anger
Ephesians 5:1–21: Imitating God
Ephesians 6:10–20: The Great Conflict
The book of Philippians
Philippians 1:12: What's Happening to Your Happenings?
Philippians 2:3: Humility
Philippians 3:13–14: Forgetting the Past
Colossians 3:1–17: Cleaning Up Your Life
1 Timothy 5:17: Honoring the Elders
1 Timothy 6:11: Fleeing and Pursuing
2 Timothy 2: An Approved Workman
2 Timothy 2:24–25: Ministerial Conduct
Hebrews 3:12–14: Taking Care; Encouragement
Hebrews 4:14–16: Jesus Understands
Hebrews 10:19–25: Holding Fast in Hope
Hebrews 12:1–5: Running to Win and Endure
Hebrews 13:7, 17: Imitate and Obey Your Leaders
James 3:2, 6: We All Stumble; The Tongue
1 Peter 2:1–12: God's Gift of Oneness in Christ
1 Peter 2:9–10: From Darkness to Light
1 Peter 3:8–12; 4:7–11: Living in Harmony
1 Peter 5:1–5: Caring for the Flock
1 Peter 5:6–7: Handling Conflict
1 John 1:9: Cleansing, Forgiveness
1 John 2:1–2: What About Our Sins?
1 John 3:1–3: God's Great Love
1 John 4:7: Loving One Another
1 John 5:1–5: Faith and Love
Revelation 2–3: Strengths and Weaknesses
Revelation 21–22: The Final Victory

Notes

Chapter 1

1. Louis Berkhof, *Systematic Theology* (Grand Rapids: Eerdmans, 1949), 610.

2. Peter Eldersveld, *Our Preaching and Our World* (Christian Reformed Minister's Institute, printed speeches, June 6–8, 1961), 29.

3. The epistles are homiletical in nature, especially the latter part of Paul's letters. In this sense they are sermons. John A. Broadus calls them sermons in his book, *The Preparation and Delivery of Sermons,* rev. ed. (New York: Harper Bros., 1944), 36–37.

Chapter 2

1. This is based on a questionnaire sent to 500 pastors in fourteen denominations, 75 percent of whom responded with this information.

2. Harold Pierce, interview with author, Southern Baptist Church, Artesia, California.

3. H. Beecher Hicks, Jr., *Preaching Through a Storm* (Grand Rapids: Zondervan, 1987), 12.

4. James Stalker, *The Preacher and His Models* (New York: Hunt & Eaton, 1892), 167.

Chapter 4

1. *Rocky Mountain News,* Denver, 5 April 1985, 8.

2. Survey of 500 churches in the United States and Canada, "Causes of Trauma."

3. The sermon has been abridged to fit the purpose of this chapter.

4. Anthony Hoekema, *The Christian Looks at Himself* (Grand Rapids: Eerdmans, 1975), 77.

Chapter 5

1. My survey shows that the second greatest cause for conflict in the church is lack of communication between pastor, council, staff, and congregation.

2. The sermon preached on this occasion is printed later in this chapter.

3. H. Beecher Hicks, Jr., *Preaching Through a Storm* (Grand Rapids: Zondervan, 1987), 53.

4. Richard Walters, *Anger: Yours, Mine, and What to Do About It* (Grand Rapids: Zondervan, 1981).

Chapter 6

1. Charles Kemp, *Pastoral Preaching* (St. Louis: Bethany Press, 1963), 12.

2. Robert Dale, *Growing a Loving Church* (Nashville: Convention Press, 1974), 35.

3. Church Data Services has produced a computerized survey called "Church Development Survey," to be taken anonymously by the entire congregation to determine the needs of the church. It can be obtained through Denver Seminary, 3401 S. University Blvd., Englewood, CO 80110.

4. Arthur L. Teikmanis, *Preaching and Pastoral Care* (Ann Arbor, Mich.: Books on Demand, University Microfilm International 64-23551), 70.

Chapter 7

1. Speed Leas and Paul Kittlaus, *Church Fights* (Philadelphia: Westminster, 1973), 29.

2. Lewis B. Smedes, *Forgive and Forget* (San Francisco: Harper & Row, 1984), 95.

3. O. Palmer Robertson, *The Christ of the Covenants* (Phillipsburg, N.J.: Presbyterian and Reformed, 1980).

Chapter 8

1. H. Beecher Hicks, Jr., *Preaching Through a Storm* (Grand Rapids: Zondervan, 1987), 55.

2. Tryon Edwards, *Dictionary of Thoughts* (Detroit: F. B. Dickerson, 1904), 450.

3. Howard A. Snyder, *A Kingdom Manifesto* (Downers Grove, Ill.: InterVarsity Press, 1985), 12.

4. For further study of the kingdom concept I refer you to the following: Geerhardus Vos, *Jesus' Teaching on the Kingdom and the Church* (Grand Rapids: Eerdmans, 1951); and Howard A. Snyder, *The Community of the King,* (Downers Grove, Ill.: InterVarsity Press, 1977).

Chapter 9

1. John Calvin, *Institutes of the Christian Religion* (Philadelphia: Westminster, 1936), 2:503.

2. *Adiaphora* is a term (from a Greek word literally meaning "things indifferent") used to describe matters that are neither approved nor disapproved by Scripture. For example, Scripture does not render a judgment on whether it is right or wrong to purchase a television set.

3. Calvin, *Institutes of the Christian Religion,* 2:81.

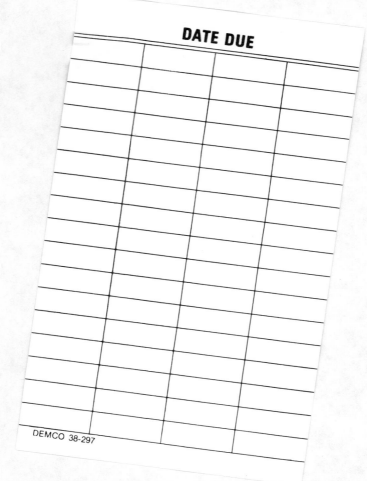

DATE DUE

DEMCO 38-297